REGENTS RESTORATION DRAMA SERIES

General Editor: John Loftis

AURENG-ZEBE

JOHN DRYDEN

Aureng-Zebe

Edited by

FREDERICK M. LINK

EDWARD ARNOLD

Cloth edition: ISBN 0 7131 5639 2
Paper edition: ISBN 0 7131 5640 6

Printed in Great Britain by
William Clowes & Sons, Limited, London, Beccles and Colchester

Regents Restoration Drama Series

The Regents Restoration Drama Series provides soundly edited texts, in modern spelling, of the more significant plays of the late seventeenth and early eighteenth centuries. The word "Restoration" is here used ambiguously and must be explained. A strict definition of the word is unacceptable to everyone, for it would exclude, among many other plays, those of Congreve. If to the historian it refers to the period between 1660 and 1685 (or 1688), it has long been used by the student of drama in default of a more precise term to refer to plays belonging to the dramatic tradition established in the 1660's, weakening after 1700, and displaced in the 1730's. It is in this extended sense—imprecise though justified by academic custom—that the word is used in this series, which includes plays first produced between 1660 and 1737. Although these limiting dates are determined by political events, the return of Charles II (and the removal of prohibitions against operation of theaters) and the passage of Walpole's Stage Licensing Act, they enclose a period of dramatic history having a coherence of its own in the establishment, development, and disintegration of a tradition.

The editors have planned the series with attention to the projected dimensions of the completed whole, a representative collection of Restoration drama providing a record of artistic achievement and providing also a record of the deepest concerns of three generations of Englishmen. And thus it contains deservedly famous plays—*The Country Wife*, *The Man of Mode*, and *The Way of the World*—and also significant but little known plays, *The Virtuoso*, for example, and *City Politiques*, the former a satirical review of scientific investigation in the early years of the Royal Society, the latter an equally satirical review of politics at the time of the Popish Plot. If the volumes of famous plays finally achieve the larger circulation, the other volumes may conceivably have the greater utility, in making available texts otherwise difficult of access with the editorial apparatus needed to make them intelligible.

The editors have had the instructive example of the parallel and senior project, the Regents Renaissance Drama Series; they have in fact used the editorial policies developed for the earlier plays as their own, modifying them as appropriate for the later period and as the experience of successive editions suggested. The introductions to the separate Restoration plays differ considerably in their nature. Although a uniform body of relevant information is presented in each of them, no attempt has been made to impose a pattern of interpretation. Emphasis in the introductions has necessarily varied with the nature of the plays and inevitably—we think desirably— with the special interests and aptitudes of the different editors.

Each text in the series is based on a fresh collation of the seventeenth- and eighteenth-century editions that might be presumed to have authority. The textual notes, which appear above the rule at the bottom of each page, record all substantive departures from the edition used as the copy-text. Variant substantive readings among contemporary editions are listed there as well. Editions later than the eighteenth century are referred to in the textual notes only when an emendation originating in some one of them is received into the text. Variants of accidentals (spelling, punctuation, capitalization) are not recorded in the notes except in instances in which they have, or may have, substantive relevance. Contracted forms of characters' names are silently expanded in speech prefixes and stage directions and, in the case of speech prefixes, are regularized. Additions to the stage directions of the copy-text are enclosed in brackets.

Spelling has been modernized along consciously conservative lines, but within the limits of a modernized text the linguistic quality of the original has been carefully preserved. Contracted preterites have regularly been expanded. Punctuation has been brought into accord with modern practices. The objective has been to achieve a balance between the pointing of the old editions and a system of punctuation which, without overloading the text with exclamation marks, semicolons, and dashes, will make the often loosely flowing verse and prose of the original syntactically intelligible to the modern reader. Dashes are regularly used only to indicate interrupted speeches, or shifts of address within a single speech.

Explanatory notes, chiefly concerned with glossing obsolete words and phrases, are printed below the textual notes at the bottom of each page. References to stage directions in the notes follow the admirable system of the Revels editions, whereby stage directions are keyed, decimally, to the line of the text before or after which they occur. Thus, a note on 0.2 has reference to the second line of the stage direction at the beginning of the scene in question. A note on 115.1 has reference to the first line of the stage direction following line 115 of the text of the relevant scene. Speech prefixes, and any stage directions attached to them, are keyed to the first line of accompanying dialogue.

JOHN LOFTIS

Stanford University

Contents

List of Abbreviations

Beaurline-Bowers	John Dryden. *Four Tragedies*. Ed. L. A. Beaurline and Fredson Bowers. Chicago, 1967.
OED	*The Oxford English Dictionary*
om.	omitted
Q1	Quarto 1 (1676)
Q2	Quarto 2 (1685)
Q3	Quarto 3 (1690)
Q4	Quarto 4 (1692)
Q5	Quarto 5 (1694)
Q6	Quarto 6 (1699)
S.D.	stage direction
S.P.	speech prefix
Scott-Saintsbury	*The Works of John Dryden*. Ed. Sir Walter Scott. Revised George Saintsbury. Vol. V. Edinburgh, 1883.

Introduction

Aureng-Zebe was entered in the Stationers' Register on November 29, 1675;[1] the first edition, printed for Henry Herringman, was advertised for sale in the *London Gazette* for February 17–21, 1676, and recorded in the Term Catalogue for Easter Term (May 5) of that year.[2] Five additional quartos appeared during Dryden's lifetime: in 1685, 1690, 1692, 1694, and 1699. Of these, Q3 (1690) is the most corrupt, but all are derivative and none bears any sign of authorial correction or change. Q3 and Q6 (1699) add a subtitle, "The Great Mogul," which appears in the Register entry but not in the other quartos. The play was reprinted several times in the eighteenth and nineteenth centuries, most notably in Sir Walter Scott's edition of Dryden; recently, it has been edited by L. A. Beaurline and Fredson Bowers for the collection *John Dryden: Four Tragedies*.[3]

The copy-text for the present edition is a quarto of 1675 in the Folger Library. With it I have collated other copies of Q1 in the Harvard, Texas, Newberry, Yale, and Huntington Libraries, and two copies each of the other five quartos. I found no press variants among Q1 copies. The few changes from copy-text which I have admitted are cited in the textual notes at the foot of the appropriate page, along with the substantive variants found in Q2–6. The latter have no authority, but may be historically useful.

Modernizing the punctuation of a play written in rhymed couplets

---

[1] "Master Henry Herringman entered for his copy under the hands of Master Roger L'Estrange and Master Warden Macock a book or copy entitled *Aureng-Zebe, or The Great Mogul*, written by John Dryden, servant to his Majesty" (*A Transcript of the Registers of the Worshipful Company of Stationers from 1640–1708 A.D.* [London, 1914], III, 12). Here, and in all other quotations, I have modernized capitalization, spelling, and punctuation.

[2] "*Aureng-Zebe*. A tragedy, acted at the Theatre Royal. Written by John Dryden, servant to his Majesty. In quarto. Stitched, 1s. Printed for Henry Herringman in the New Exchange" (*The Term Catalogues, 1668–1709*, ed. Edward Arber [London, 1903], I, 236).

[3] Professor Beaurline kindly allowed me to see the text and prefaces for his edition in advance of publication.

necessarily interposes the arbitrary decisions of an editor between author and reader. *Aureng-Zebe* is heavily pointed, often in ways not clear to a reader today. I have reduced the number of commas, and have used other marks as often as possible in their modern sense. Q1 is thoroughly inconsistent in the matter of contraction for metrical purposes. Forms like *pow'r* and *Heav'n* regularly appear, but not invariably; *bus'ness* is once uncontracted, *generous* is once contracted. I have retained the readings of the copy-text.

The first recorded performance of *Aureng-Zebe* took place on Wednesday, November 17, 1675, at the Theatre Royal in Drury Lane.[4] It was played again on the following Saturday, and on November 29 at Court. No further seventeenth-century performances are known, but since the play was acted several times between 1705 and 1727, it is possible that the later quarto editions reflect revivals.[5]

The play was not as popular in the early years of the eighteenth century as *The Indian Emperor*, and certainly was not acted as often as *All for Love* and *The Spanish Friar*. *The London Stage* lists ten performances 1700–1710, fourteen 1711–1720, ten 1721–1730, and only one thereafter, though an altered version was produced at Covent Garden as late as 1774, with the title *The Prince of Agra*. Most of the performances early in the century took place at Drury Lane. On February 19, 1708, for example, Betterton acted the part of the Emperor, Booth that of Morat; Powell played Aureng-Zebe, and Mrs. Barry, Indamora. On December 12, 1721, Wilks acted Aureng-Zebe to Mrs. Oldfield's Indamora; Booth again played Morat. It is clear, however, that the play, like many others of its type and time, was out of fashion long before the Licensing Act of 1737.

Dryden based his play on François Bernier's account of the struggle of the four sons of Shah Jahan, fifth Mogul emperor, for the succession to the throne. Bernier's book, *Histoire de la dernière révolution des états du Grand Mogul*, was published in 1670, with a sequel in 1671. Both were translated into English almost immediately, in 1671

---

[4] My information about the stage history of the play comes from the volumes of *The London Stage*, ed. Emmett L. Avery, Arthur H. Scouten, *et al.* (Carbondale, Ill., 1960–1968), which incorporate earlier scholarship.

[5] An advertisement for the performance at Drury Lane on February 19, 1708, reads "not acted there these thirteen years"; and though such statements are not always accurate, this information is consistent with the date of Q5. See *The London Stage*, Pt. 2, Vol. I, p. 426.

and 1672 respectively. The play is thus about recent events in India, distant enough from Dryden's audience in space to permit him considerable latitude in constructing a plot. He used the latitude fully. The changes and additions he made show his craftsmanship, and reveal the essential features of his design.

The initial situation is taken over directly. Bernier describes it (in the English translation Dryden presumably used):

> I found also at my arrival that this king of the world, Shah Jahan, of above seventy years of age, had four sons and two daughters; that some years since he had made these four sons vice-kings or governors of four of his most considerable provinces or kingdoms; that it was almost a year that he was fallen into a great sickness, whence it was believed he would never recover: which had occasioned a great division among these four brothers (all laying claim to the empire), and had kindled among them a war which lasted five years. . . .[6]

Dryden has changed only the "all laying claim," excepting Aureng-Zebe from the charge.

The place names and the names of the Emperor and the four sons are historical. Bernier mentions in passing the names Dianet and Fazel Khan. Dryden takes over from him the names Abas, Solyman, Mir Baba, and Nourmahal, but their roles in the play are Dryden's creation. Nourmahal, for example, was in fact the wife of Shah Jahan's father; Solyman was Darah's eldest son. Many incidental details in the play come from the *History:* the false report of the Emperor's death and the pretense that his assurances to the contrary are forgeries; the embassy to the Emperor; the poust, or death by slow poison; the self-immolation of Melesinda; and probably the association of Indamora with Kashmir, a country, according to Bernier, remarkable for the beauty of its women. Even so, Dryden often alters either detail or context: Bernier mentions the poust in connection with the death of Solyman; Melesinda was Mohammedan and therefore would not have followed the Hindu custom of suttee.

Many of the changes are the natural result of simplifying a complex intrigue among four brothers into a single action in which Aureng-Zebe opposes Morat, and of compressing the time from several years into a single critical day. Thus, the rout of Darah and

[6] *The History of the Late Revolution of the Empire of the Great Mogul* (London, 1671), [B3ᵛ]–B4.

Sujah, which historically spanned several years, is in the play accomplished by consecutive victories of Aureng-Zebe reported early in the first act. The important changes, however, result from Dryden's conception of his central figure. He wished to present a hero who would compel the admiration of his audience, and whose valor and virtue would be rewarded with power and love.[7] The historical Aureng-Zebe did not meet these requirements. Bernier describes him thus:

> Aureng-Zebe . . . had not that gallantry nor surprising presence of Darah; he appeared more serious and melancholy, and was indeed much more judicious, understanding the world very well, and knowing whom to choose for his service and purpose. . . . He was reserved, crafty, and exceedingly versed in dissembling, insomuch that for a long while he made profession to be fakir, that is, poor, dervish, or devout, renouncing the world and feigning not to pretend at all to the crown, but to desire to pass his life in prayer and other devotion. [C1^v]

Bernier excuses him in part by reference to the Mogul habit of settling the succession by bloodshed, and in fact tells his reader that if he reflects he will not take the new Emperor for "a barbarian, but for a great and rare genius, a great statesman, and a great king" ([Mm1^v]). But he believes that "most of those who shall have read my history will judge the ways taken by Aureng-Zebe for getting the empire very violent and horrid" ([Mm1]).

The distinguishing traits in Bernier's portrait are cleverness and deviousness; Aureng-Zebe won the war more through diplomacy and uncommon luck than by force of arms. Furthermore, he usurped the throne, imprisoned his father, duped Morat, and in one way or another murdered Morat, Darah, Solyman, Morat's grandson, and the entire family of Sujah.

But he had won the war, and he was still Emperor when Dryden came to write his play. Therefore, Dryden had to remake him. In the first place, he could not usurp the throne; he would not then be virtuous, and the ferment in the England of 1675 over the succession would have made the overthrow of the legitimate monarch by a

---

[7] For further discussion of this point, see Michael Alssid, "The Design of Dryden's *Aureng-Zebe*," *Journal of English and Germanic Philology*, LXIV (1965), 452–469. This essay is one of the best studies of the play, particularly of its imagery.

younger son a dangerous subject for a play, and certainly one foreign to Dryden's political convictions. Aureng-Zebe is therefore separated from the other brothers. He fights for the Emperor rather than for himself, defends his father though betrayed by him, opposes rather than joins Morat, and receives the crown legitimately at the end of the play.

Secondly, his moral defects had to be eliminated. Dryden makes him direct and honest to the point of artlessness, ignoring the hypocrisy stressed by Bernier, his treachery to Morat, and all the murders for which he was responsible. Dryden emphasizes his valor and judgment, and conversely minimizes the virtues Bernier attributes to his brothers. Darah is seen in the *History* as a complex and even tragic figure; Dryden dismisses him in four lines. He transforms Sujah into a bigot controlled by a foreign power, and Morat into a bravo whose very bravery is undercut in the course of the play.

Finally, Aureng-Zebe must be rewarded with private as well as public success, with love as well as power. Bernier could be of no use here. Dryden therefore invented Indamora,[8] and with characteristic economy used her to estrange Aureng-Zebe from his father and thus produce the necessary blocking action, and to develop and test both father and son.

The hero, then, is endowed with virtue and with love at the very start of the play. *Aureng-Zebe* is not an exploration of character developing through inner conflict toward self-knowledge, but a play demonstrating the proper conduct of a prince. We are not to identify with the hero as a realistic figure; we are to admire him as an ideal, as the paradigm of a governor. He is essentially a static character in the political action of the play: the major obstacles he must overcome are external, and the events of the play illustrate his character rather than develop from it. The structure, by consequence, is episodic, designed to exhibit the behavior of the hero under various stresses in both public and private roles. The outcome of the testing is never seriously in doubt, though Aureng-Zebe shows enough uncertainty and weakness—particularly in his relationship with Indamora—to make him a believable rather than a mechanical pattern.

A brief examination of the central action will demonstrate Dryden's method. Even in the opening scene the Omrahs comment on the

8 Alssid's suggestion ("The Design of Dryden's *Aureng-Zebe*," p. 455) that Indamora may stand for love of India is thematically plausible, and the name is not found in Bernier's *History*.

age and helplessness of the Emperor, and see Aureng-Zebe as the Atlas who will uphold "our sinking state." In return, he may expect "a parent's blessing and a mistress' love": expectations the Omrahs deem natural and just. The Emperor, in denying them, sets the plot in motion, and simultaneously reveals that he is no longer fit to rule. He has neither power nor wisdom; he can control neither his country nor his own emotions. Since he is Emperor, however, and since Aureng-Zebe's loyalty to him must have some credibility, he is made pitiable rather than vicious. His arrogance is bluster: he knows he is reprehensible, and struggles periodically against his infatuation with Indamora.

Aureng-Zebe's behavior, by contrast, is exemplary. He is astonished by his father's reception of him, but affirms his loyalty and obedience nevertheless. His first important test comes when he confronts an altered Indamora, and forces from her an acknowledgment of his father's infatuation. His initial display of anger humanizes him, and it emphasizes his courage and the strength of his love. When Indamora reminds him of his duty, however, he quickly reveals the ability to control his resentment. His comment at this point must puzzle those who have seen Dryden's heroic drama as the celebration of romantic individualism:

> I've thought, and blessed be you who gave me time;
> My virtue was surprised into a crime.
> Strong virtue, like strong nature, struggles still,
> Exerts itself, and then throws off the ill. (I.461–464)

As the action is further complicated, Aureng-Zebe defeats Morat and saves Nourmahal from his father's anger. The Emperor, deeper in his son's debt, again shows his inability to control himself; the son shows his superior statesmanship and virtue. The confrontation over Indamora, delayed until this point for maximum suspense, now follows. Aureng-Zebe claims her "as your general and your son," firmly withstanding the Emperor's appeals and threats. His father flies into a guilty rage, and acts to destroy himself by admitting Morat into the Citadel. Aureng-Zebe's dilemma is acute. He must remain loyal both as subject and son, yet he realizes that his father's irrationality is ruinous to them both. He can control himself, but not the outside world. Again Dryden humanizes his hero, this time by having him question the code he lives by. At first he puts his choice in selfish terms: "I'll not betray the glory of my name." When Dianet argues that "Honor which only does the name advance/ Is the mere raving madness of romance," Aureng-Zebe answers obliquely, but shifts to ground more defensible in a prince: he will appeal to Morat's honor, the most diplomatic course. The aphorism which ends the act shows him once more steadfast against temptation: "Presence of mind and courage in distress/ Are more than armies to procure success."

As Act III begins, the Emperor, like Lear, has endangered his kingdom to gratify himself, and Morat is temporarily in power. The contrast between the brothers is at once made apparent. Aureng-Zebe has shown concern for the people, whom Morat calls "stiff-necked animals" to be kept on a tight rein. Aureng-Zebe has revealed himself as a statesman, Morat as an easily led would-be conqueror impatient for self-glorification. The confrontation between the two establishes the former's moral superiority: despite Aureng-Zebe's initial self-righteousness, his proposals to Morat expose the latter even to the Emperor, who fails once more to throw off his infatuation with Indamora.

In the remainder of the act, two further temptations are prepared for Aureng-Zebe. Nourmahal reveals to Zayda her incestuous desire for him, and Morat deserts his wife for Indamora. Act IV exploits for sensational purposes Nourmahal's efforts to seduce the hero; though Aureng-Zebe faces immediate death, one cannot seriously believe that she will be successful. More important is the threat she poses to his belief in the meaning and value of life, a belief already shaken by the actions of his father. It is at this point that he considers life a "cheat," and momentarily despairs. He resists his stepmother with horror, but is nearly overwhelmed by his jealousy of Morat.

Between Morat's taunt to his brother and the presentation of its effect Dryden skilfully interposes two further examples of Morat's lack of principle: Morat discards his wife and betrays his father. Nevertheless, Aureng-Zebe is not seen to advantage when he confronts Indamora. His behavior is partially justified, because Indamora has temporized with Morat (though not to the extent he assumes), and she does behave imperiously. But he indulges his anger, and he does not demonstrate the magnanimity expected in a prince or a lover.[9]

9 Although the two scenes between Aureng-Zebe and Indamora, and the latter's exchanges with Arimant, suggest the influence of contemporary comedy, I cannot agree with Bruce King (*Dryden's Major Plays* [New York, 1966], Chapter 7) that the audience is to take scene, character, or play as

In the end, his jealousy is submerged in his passion rather than subordinated to his reason.

His forgiveness of his father, however, does illustrate magnanimity: it occurs when the fortunes of both are at their lowest ebb. The "conversion" of Morat, which follows, is perhaps as improbable as the Emperor's infatuation at the age of seventy, but one must keep in mind the dramatic convention of love playing havoc with psychological plausibility. It is more relevant to look at what Dryden accomplishes by this "turn" and by Morat's death. He displays Indamora's power even more strongly than in the Arimant scenes; he motivates Aureng-Zebe's final attack of jealousy and yet leaves him guiltless of bloodshed, in sole possession of Indamora, and heir to the throne; he prepares for Melesinda's sensational exit; and he motivates Nourmahal's even more sensational madness and suicide.

Thematically the focus remains on Aureng-Zebe. He takes instant command in the crisis, and his first orders affirm his moral right to do so; he offers amnesty to all, and decrees an end to the rule of fratricide. The second trial of his love is enough to stagger him, but he controls his feelings until he is alone with Indamora, and offers to leave without venting them. His outburst this time is briefer, and soon turns into argument. When she leaves, he acknowledges her innocence and belatedly goes to call her back. He has met his final test, not perfectly, but well enough to show that his jealousy is also subject to control. It is only fitting that it is the Emperor who brings Indamora back to him, resigning to his son in one couplet both love and power:

> Receive the mistress you so long have served;
> Receive the crown your loyalty preserved.
>
> (V.671–672)

Aureng-Zebe is therefore didactic in the sense that it exemplifies a political ideal. I have chosen to stress what might be considered the public character of the play, partly because the serious drama of the Restoration is sometimes considered merely sensational, partly because such an interpretation avoids overemphasis on the exoticism

---

comic in any important sense. Although Indamora's scene with Arimant develops a side of her character which relates her to the heroines of wit comedy, it has important thematic functions which have nothing to do with comedy.

of the heroic play, and partly because structure and characterization can thereby be explained as natural consequences of a rhetorical intention.

The rhetorical purpose is everywhere apparent. It lies behind the elaborate diction and imagery, behind the formal, distanced pattern of the lines. When the Emperor reports to Arimant the failure of his suit to Indamora, we do not get the anguish of disappointed and futile passion, but a carefully articulated comparison:

> Unmoved she stood, and deaf to all my prayers,
> As seas and winds to sinking mariners.
> But seas grow calm, and winds are reconciled;
> Her tyrant beauty never grows more mild.
>
> (I.266–269)

When Aureng-Zebe is at the height of passion, the language becomes more informal and the rhythms more turbulent, but the distance and the sense of calculated art remain:

> Ah, traitress! Ah, ingrate! Ah, faithless mind!
> Ah, sex invented first to damn mankind!
> Nature took care to dress you up for sin:
> Adorned without, unfinished left within.
> Hence by no judgment you your loves direct;
> Talk much, ne'er think, and still the wrong affect.
> So much self-love in your composures mixed
> That love to others still remains unfixed.
> Greatness and noise and show are your delight,
> Yet wise men love you in their own despite;
> And finding in their native wit no ease,
> Are forced to put your folly on to please.
>
> (IV.ii.100–111)

To say that this is not the language of the heart is to miss the point.

Elaborate pattern is also evident in the contrast of characters. Melesinda's supine meekness sets off Indamora's active nature; at the other extreme from Melesinda is Nourmahal. Morat's naïveté emphasizes Aureng-Zebe's diplomacy; his hot-headedness accentuates his brother's superior control. Arimant's love for Indamora provides contrast with the Emperor's; both loves are hopeless, but one leads to noble, the other to ignoble, conduct. The movement of

the plot involves constant turn and counterturn. Melesinda con-
gratulates Indamora on her good fortune, but in an hour their
situations are reversed. Morat embraces his wife only to cast her off
a scene or two later.

Dryden's handling of dialogue indicates both his interest in
complex design and his rhetorical intent. More than 1,900 of the
play's 2,869 lines are spoken by two characters in conversation. A
third character is often on stage primarily to effect a transition
without breaking the continuous scene. A common pattern is A–B,
enter C, A–B–C, exit B, A–C (II.31–202; III.396–558). Occasionally
the emphasis on dialogue is even stronger. In Act I the Emperor
has successive conversations with Morat's ambassador, Arimant, and
Aureng-Zebe; only after the third does the focus shift to the son.
Act V and both scenes in Act IV begin with long dialogues, and Act
III with a shorter one. In fact, the important exchange at III.190–327
is the only one in the play before the middle of Act V when more than
three principals talk together, and even here more than a third of the
lines involve interchange between Aureng-Zebe and Morat.

Furthermore, many of the dialogues are forensic. The Emperor
explores with Arimant passion's control of his reason (I.184–293);
Aureng-Zebe persuades Indamora to tell her secret (I.354–438);
Indamora bends Arimant to her will (II.39–113); the Emperor
debates possession of Indamora with his son (II.376–513); the two
lovers argue whether her behavior and his jealousy are justifiable
(IV.ii.7–159 and V.439–575). Although Morat and Nourmahal die
on stage, and battles and rumors of battles are frequently reported,
the "action" of the play is thus largely verbal. As the moral issues
are debated and resolved, the external action is brought into line:
Arimant's stratagem works, the fort revolts to the Emperor, Morat's
conversion rewards Indamora's virtue and saves her life, and so on.

In the dedication Dryden somewhat humorously remarks that his
female characters are more realistic than their counterparts in the
French heroic romances. He is not suggesting that these works are
his sources; his point is that made again by Dr. Johnson a century
later, in his life of Pope: "Narrations of romantic and impracticable
virtue will be read with wonder, but that which is unattainable is
recommended in vain; that good may be endeavored, it must be
shown to be possible." Studies of the heroic play have derived the
form from sources as various as Caroline court drama, French romance,
Racine and Corneille, Tasso and Ariosto, and Beaumont and Flet-

cher.[10] And indeed, a case can be made for all these, so long as the plays are not seen as rigid conflicts of love and honor, celebrations of Byronism, or philosophical commentaries on Plato, Epicurus, Descartes, and Hobbes; and so long as one takes into account the great differences among particular examples of the form.[11] Dryden's insistence that the classical and Renaissance epics were his models is primary. The concept of epic in the period explains the nature of the hero, the episodic and often coincidental structure, the elevated rhetoric, and the public—often political—theme interwoven with the love story. Aureng-Zebe was Dryden's last rhymed play, and it is also his best, not only in sureness of design and richness of language, but in the economy of its plot and the thematic relevance of its strands of action.

FREDERICK M. LINK

University of Nebraska

---

10 The commentary on *The Indian Queen* in *The Works of John Dryden*, Vol. VIII, ed. J. H. Smith, Dougald MacMillan, *et al.* (Berkeley and Los Angeles, 1962), succinctly summarizes the various theories and gives appropriate citations.

11 Relevant modern studies of particular usefulness include Arthur C. Kirsch, *Dryden's Heroic Drama* (Princeton, 1965), and Eric Rothstein, *Restoration Tragedy* (Madison, 1967).

AURENG-ZEBE

To the Right Honorable John, Earl of Mulgrave,
Gentlemen of His Majesty's Bedchamber,
and Knight of the Most Noble Order of the Garter.

MY LORD,

'Tis a severe reflection which Montaigne has made on
princes, that we ought not, in reason, to have any expectations of favor from them; and that 'tis kindness enough if
they leave us in possession of our own. The boldness of the   5
censure shows the free spirit of the author, and the subjects
of England may justly congratulate to themselves that both
the nature of our government and the clemency of our king
secure us from any such complaint. I, in particular, who
subsist wholly by his bounty, am obliged to give posterity   10
a far other account of my royal master that what Montaigne
has left of his. Those accusations had been more reasonable
if they had been placed on inferior persons. For in all courts
there are too many who make it their business to ruin wit,
and Montaigne in other places tells us what effects he found   15
of their good natures. He describes them such, whose ambition, lust, or private interest seem to be the only end of their
creation. If good accrue to any from them, 'tis only in order
to their own designs: conferred most commonly on the base
and infamous, and never given, but only *hap'ning* sometimes   20
on well deservers. Dulness has brought them to what they
are, and malice secures them in their fortunes. But somewhat of specious they must have to recommend themselves
to princes, for folly will not easily go down in its own
natural form with discerning judges. And diligence in   25
waiting is their gilding of the pill, for that looks like love,

10. by] *Q 1–2, 4–6*; upon *Q 3*.   19. their own] *Q 1–2*; own their
                                          Q 3–6.

0.1.] John Sheffield, Earl of Mulgrave (1648–1721), was a poet and
critic as well as Dryden's patron.

2–5. *Montaigne . . . own*] in *Essays* III. ix, "Of Vanity."

9–10. *I . . . bounty*] Dryden was at this time poet laureate and historiographer royal.

15. *in other places*] *Essays* III. i, "Of Utility and Honesty."

though 'tis only interest. 'Tis that which gains 'em their advantage over witty men, whose love of liberty and ease makes them willing too often to discharge their burden of attendance on these officious gentlemen. 'Tis true that the 30 nauseousness of such company is enough to disgust a reasonable man, when he sees he can hardly approach greatness but as a moated castle; he must first pass through the mud and filth with which it is encompassed. These are they who, wanting wit, affect gravity, and go by the name of solid men; 35 and a solid man is, in plain English, a solid, solemn fool. Another disguise they have (for fools as well as knaves take other names, and pass by an alias), and that is the title of honest fellows. But this honesty of theirs ought to have many grains for its allowance, for certainly they are no farther 40 honest than they are silly. They are naturally mischievous to their power, and if they speak not maliciously or sharply of witty men, 'tis only because God has not bestowed on them the gift of utterance. They fawn and crouch to men of parts, whom they cannot ruin; quote their wit when they 45 are present, and when they are absent steal their jests. But to those who are under 'em, and whom they can crush with ease, they show themselves in their natural antipathy; there they treat wit like the common enemy, and give it no more quarter than a Dutchman would to an English vessel in the 50 Indies; they strike sail where they know they shall be mastered, and murder where they can with safety.

This, my Lord, is the character of a courtier without wit, and therefore that which is a satire to other men must be a panegyric to your Lordship, who are a master of it. 55 If the least of these reflections could have reached your person, no necessity of mine could have made me to have sought so earnestly and so long to have cultivated your kindness. As a poet, I cannot but have made some observations on mankind; the lowness of my fortune has not yet 60 brought me to flatter vice, and 'tis my duty to give testimony to virtue. 'Tis true your Lordship is not of that nature which

---

30. these] *Q 1–2, 4–6*; those *Q 3*.   46. jests] *Q 1–3*; jest *Q 4–6*.

50. *Dutchman*] The recent Dutch wars had been occasioned in part by commercial rivalries.

either seeks a commendation or want it. Your mind has
always been above the wretched affectation of popularity.
A popular man is, in truth, no better than a prostitute to   65
common fame and to the people. He lies down to everyone
he meets for the hire of praise, and his humility is only a
disguised ambition. Even Cicero himself, whose eloquence
deserved the admiration of mankind; yet by his insatiable
thirst of fame he has lessened his character with succeeding   70
ages. His action against Catiline may be said to have ruined
the consul when it saved the city, for it so swelled his soul,
which was not truly great, that ever afterwards it was apt
to be overset with vanity. And this made his virtue so sus-
pected by his friends that Brutus, whom of all men he adored,   75
refused him a place in his conspiracy. A modern wit has
made this observation on him, that coveting to recommend
himself to posterity, he begged it as an alms of all his friends
the historians, to remember his consulship: and observe if
you please the oddness of the event; all their histories are   80
lost, and the vanity of his request stands yet recorded in
his own writings. How much more great and manly in your
Lordship is your contempt of popular applause and your
retired virtue, which shines only to a few; with whom you
live so easily and freely that you make it evident you have a   85
soul which is capable of all the tenderness of friendship, and
that you only retire yourself from those who are not capable
of returning it. Your kindness, where you have once placed
it, is inviolable, and 'tis to that only I attribute my happiness in your love. This makes me more easily forsake an   90
argument on which I could otherwise delight to dwell: I
mean your judgment in your choice of friends; because I
have the honor to be one. After which, I am sure you will
more easily permit me to be silent, in the care you have taken

63. either] *Q 1–2, 4–6*; neither *Q 3*.   80. all] *Q 1–2, 4–5*; *om. Q 3*; and
63. want] *Q 1–2, 4–6*; wants *Q 3*.   *Q 6*.
67. meets] *Q 1–2, 4–6*; meet *Q 3*.

71–72. *Catiline . . . consul*] Cicero, consul in 63 B.C., put down the insur-
rection led by Catiline, and prosecuted its leaders.
76. *conspiracy*] to assassinate Julius Caesar.
76. *wit*] Montaigne (*Essays* I. xl, "A Consideration upon Cicero").
82. *writings*] in a letter to Lucceius (*Epistolae ad familiares* V. xii).

of my fortune, which you have rescued, not only from the 95
power of others, but from my worst of enemies, my own
modesty and laziness. Which favor, had it been employed on
a more deserving subject, had been an effect of justice in
your nature; but, as placed on me, is only charity. Yet
withal, 'tis conferred on such a man as prefers your kindness 100
itself before any of its consequences, and who values as the
greatest of your favors, those of your love and of your conversation. From this constancy to your friends I might
reasonably assume that your resentments would be as strong
and lasting, if they were not restrained by a nobler principle 105
of good nature and generosity. For certainly, 'tis the same
composition of mind, the same resolution and courage,
which makes the greatest friendships, and the greatest
enmities. And he who is too lightly reconciled after high
provocations may recommend himself to the world for a 110
Christian, but I should hardly trust him for a friend. The
Italians have a proverb to that purpose: "To forgive the
first time shows me a good Catholic, the second time a fool."
To this firmness in all your actions (though you are wanting
in no other ornaments of mind and body, yet to this) I 115
principally ascribe the interest your merits have acquired you
in the royal family. A prince who is constant to himself
and steady in all his undertakings; one with whom that
character of Horace will agree:

Si fractus illabatur orbis   120
impavidum serient ruinae.

Such a one cannot but place an esteem and repose a confidence on him whom no adversity, no change of courts, no
bribery of interests, or cabals of factions, or advantages of
fortune, can remove from the solid foundations of honor and 125
fidelity.

96. power] *Q 1–2, 4–6*; powers *Q 3.*   118. undertakings] *Q 1–2, 4–6*;
102–103. of your conversation]   undertaking *Q 3.*
Q 1–2, 4–6; your conversation *Q 3.*   124. interests] *Q 1–2, 4–5*; interest
                                            Q 3, 6.

120–121.] *Carminum* III. iii, verse 2: "Should the whole frame of nature
round him break,/ In ruin and confusion hurled,/ He, unconcerned, would
hear the mighty crack,/ And stand secure amidst a falling world" (trans.
Addison).

Ille meos, primus qui me sibi junxit, amores
abstulit; ille habeat secum servetque sepulcro.

How well your Lordship will deserve that praise, I need
no inspiration to foretell. You have already left no room 130
for prophecy: your early undertakings have been such, in
the service of your king and country (when you offered
yourself to the most dangerous employment, that of the sea;
when you chose to abandon those delights to which your
youth and fortune did invite you to undergo the hazards 135
and, which was worse, the company of common seamen),
that you have made it evident you will refuse no opportunity
of rend'ring yourself useful to the nation when either your
courage or conduct shall be required. The same zeal and
faithfulness continues in your blood which animated one of 140
your noble ancestors to sacrifice his life in the quarrel of
his sovereign, though I hope, both for your sake and for the
public tranquility, the same occasion will never be offered
to your Lordship, and that a better destiny will attend you.
But I make haste to consider you as abstracted from a 145
court which (if you will give me leave to use a term of logic)
is only an adjunct, not a propriety of happiness. The Academics, I confess, were willing to admit the goods of fortune
into their notion of felicity, but I do not remember that
any of the sects of old philosophers did ever leave a room 150
for greatness. Neither am I formed to praise a court, who
admire and covet nothing but the easiness and quiet of
retirement. I naturally withdraw my sight from a precipice;
and admit the prospect be never so large and goodly, can
take no pleasure even in looking on the downfall, though I 155

---

143. will] *Q 1-2, 4-6; om. Q 3.*   155. downfall] *Q 1, 3, 4-6; downful*
                                              Q 2.

127–128.] *Aeneid* IV. 28–29: "No! He who had my vows, shall ever
have;/ For whom I loved on earth, I worship in the grave" (trans. Dryden).
   133. *employment*] The earl had served with such distinction as a naval
volunteer in the Dutch war of 1672–1674 that he was given his own command.
   140–141. *one ... ancestors*] An earlier Lord Sheffield had been killed in the
Catholic riots of 1548–1549 (Scott).
   147. *adjunct*] a non-essential property.
   147–148. *Academics*] followers of the school of Plato.

am secure from the danger. Methinks there's something of
a malignant joy in that excellent description of Lucretius:

> Suave, mari magno turbantibus aequora ventis,
> e terra magnum alterius spectare laborem;
> non quia vexari quenquam est jucunda voluptas,   160
> sed quibus ipse malis careas quia cernere suave est.

I am sure his master Epicurus, and my better master
Cowley, preferred the solitude of a garden and the conversation of a friend to any consideration, so much as a
regard, of those unhappy people whom in our own wrong   165
we call the great. True greatness, if it be anywhere on
earth, is in a private virtue, removed from the notion of
pomp and vanity, confined to a contemplation of itself, and
cent'ring on itself:

> Omnis enim per se divum natura, necesse est   170
> immortali aevo summa cum pace fruatur;
> .... cura semota metuque,
> ipsa suis pollens opibus ....

If this be not the life of a deity because it cannot consist
with providence, 'tis at least a godlike life; I can be con-   175
tented (and I am sure I have your Lordship of my opinion)
with an humbler station in the temple of virtue than to be
set on the pinnacle of it.

> Despicere unde queas alios passimque videre
> errare atque viam palantis quaerere vitae.   180

156. danger] Q 1–2, 4–6; dangers   175. at least] Q 1–2, 4–6; om. Q 3.
Q 3.

158–161.] De rerum natura II. 1–4: "How sweet it is, when winds are
whipping the waters on the great sea, to watch from the shore the distress
of someone else not because it is delightful that anyone be troubled, but
because it is sweet to realize from what ills you yourself are free" (transla-
tions mine unless otherwise indicated).

163. Cowley] Abraham Cowley (1618–1667) wrote a well-known essay,
The Garden (c. 1664), which celebrated the virtues of retirement.

170–173.] altered from Lucretius II. 646–650: "For it is of the very
essence of deity to enjoy immortal life in total peace, free [from care and
fear], strong in its own resources." Dryden substitutes cura metuque for all of
ll. 648–649 after semota.

179–180.] Lucretius II. 9–10: "Whence you may look down and see
others wandering to and fro, and, as they straggle, seeking a way of life."

The truth is, the consideration of so vain a creature as man is not worth our pains. I have fool enough at home without looking for it abroad, and am a sufficient theater to myself of ridiculous actions, without expecting company either in a court, a town, or playhouse. 'Tis on this account that I am 185 weary with drawing the deformities of life, and lazars of the people, where every figure of imperfection more resembles me than it can do others. If I must be condemned to rhyme, I should find some ease in my change of punishment. I desire to be no longer the Sisyphus of the stage, to roll up a stone 190 with endless labor (which, to follow the proverb, gathers no moss) and which is perpetually falling down again. I never thought myself very fit for an employment where many of my predecessors have excelled me in all kinds, and some of my contemporaries, even in my own partial judg- 195 ment, have outdone me in *comedy*. Some little hopes I have yet remaining (and those too, considering my abilities, may be vain) that I may make the world some part of amends for many ill plays by an heroic poem. Your Lordship has been long acquainted with my design, the subject of which 200 you know is great, the story English, and neither too far distant from the present age nor too near approaching it. Such it is in my opinion that I could not have wished a nobler occasion to do honor by it to my king, my country, and my friends, most of our ancient nobility being con- 205 cerned in the action. And your Lordship has one particular reason to promote this undertaking, because you were the first who gave me the opportunity of discoursing it to his Majesty and his Royal Highness; they were then pleased both to commend the design and to encourage it by their 210 commands. But the unsettledness of my condition has hitherto put a stop to my thoughts concerning it. As I am no

198. part] *Q 1–2, 4–6*; parts *Q 3*. 204. do . . . to] *Q 1–2, 4–6*; honor
200. of which] *Q 1–2, 4–6*; om. *Q 3*.   by it to do *Q 3*.
203. in] *Q 1–3*; om. *Q 4–6*.   205. my] *Q 1–4*; and *Q 5–6*.

186. *lazars*] beggars, outcasts.
190. *Sisyphus*] The story may be found in *Odyssey* xi. 593–600.
200. *subject*] Dryden says in the "Discourse concerning Satire" that the poem was to treat either King Arthur or Edward, the Black Prince.
209. *Royal Highness*] James II, then Duke of York.

successor to Homer in his wit, so neither do I desire to be in
his poverty. I can make no rhapsodies, nor go a-begging at
the Grecian doors, while I sing the praises of their ancestors. 215
The times of Vergil please me better, because he had an
Augustus for his patron. And to draw the allegory nearer you,
I am sure I shall not want a Maecenas with him. 'Tis for
your Lordship to stir up that remembrance in his Majesty,
which his many avocations of business have caused him, I 220
fear, to lay aside. And (as himself and his royal brother are
the heroes of the poem) to represent to them the images of
their warlike predecessors, as Achilles is said to be roused
to glory with the sight of the combat before the ships. For
my own part, I am satisfied to have offered the design, and 225
it may be to the advantage of my reputation to have it
refused me.

In the meantime, my Lord, I take the confidence to present you with a tragedy, the characters of which are the
nearest to those of an heroic poem. 'Twas dedicated to you 230
in my heart before 'twas presented on the stage. Some things
in it have passed your approbation, and many your amendment. You were likewise pleased to recommend it to the
King's perusal before the last hand was added to it, when I
received the favor from him to have the most considerable 235
event of it modeled by his royal pleasure. It may be some
vainty in me to add his testimony then, and which he
graciously confirmed afterwards, that it was the best of all
my tragedies, in which he has made authentic my private
opinion of it; at least, he has given it a value by his commen- 240
dation which it had not by my writing.

That which was not pleasing to some of the fair ladies
in the last act of it, as I dare not vindicate, so neither
can I wholly condemn till I find more reason for their
censures. The procedure of Indamora and Melesinda seems 245

217. nearer] *Q 1-2, 4-6*; nearer to   230. 'twas] *Q 1-2, 4-6*; it was *Q 3.*
Q 3.

214-215. *I can ... ancestors*] Tradition represented Homer as a wandering
minstrel.
218. *Maecenas*] patron of Vergil and other poets of the Augustan age.
223. *Achilles*] in the sixteenth book of the *Iliad*.

yet in my judgment natural, and not unbecoming of their
characters. If they who arraign them fail not more, the
world will never blame their conduct; and I shall be glad,
for the honor of my country, to find better images of virtue
drawn to the life in their behavior than any I could feign 250
to adorn the theater. I confess I have only represented a
practicable virtue, mixed with the frailties and imper-
fections of human life. I have made my heroine fearful of
death, which neither Cassandra nor Cleopatra would have
been; and they themselves, I doubt it not, would have out- 255
done romance in that particular. Yet their Mandana (and
the *Cyrus* was written by a lady) was not altogether so hard-
hearted, for she sat down on the cold ground by the King of
Assyria, and not only pitied him who died in her defense,
but allowed him some favors such, perhaps, as they would 260
think should only be permitted to her Cyrus. I have made
my Melesinda, in opposition to Nourmahal, a woman
passionately loving of her husband, patient of injuries and
contempt, and constant in her kindness to the last; and in
that, perhaps, I may have erred, because it is not a virtue 265
much in use. Those Indian wives are loving fools, and may
do well to keep themselves in their own country, or at least
to keep company with the Arrias and Portias of old Rome;
some of our ladies know better things. But it may be I am
partial to my own writings; yet I have labored as much as 270
any man to divest myself of the self-opinion of an author,
and am too well satisfied of my own weakness to be pleased
with anything I have written. But on the other side, my

246. unbecoming] *Q 1–2, 4–6;* be-   266. fools] *Q 1–5;* fool *Q 6.*
coming *Q 3.*

254. *Cassandra*] heroine of la Calprenède's heroic romance *Cassandre,*
trans. 1652.
254. *Cleopatra*] heroine of the same author's *Cléopatre,* trans. 1652–1658.
256. *Mandana*] heroine of Madeleine de Scudéry's *Artamène, ou le Grand
Cyrus,* trans. 1653–1655.
268. *Arrias*] Arria, wife of Caecina Paetus, killed herself as an example to
her husband (Pliny *Epistolae* III. 16).
268. *Portias*] Portia committed suicide on hearing of the death of her
husband Brutus after the battle of Philippi. The story is told in Plutarch's
life of Brutus.

reason tells me that, in probability, what I have seriously
and long considered may be as likely to be just and natural 275
as what an ordinary judge (if there be any such amongst
those ladies) will think fit, in a transient presentation, to
be placed in the room of that which they condemn. The
most judicious writer is sometimes mistaken after all his
care, but the hasty critic, who judges on a view, is full as 280
liable to be deceived. Let him first consider all the arguments which the author had to write this, or to design the
other, before he arraigns him of a fault; and then perhaps,
on second thoughts, he will find his reason oblige him to
revoke his censure. Yet, after all, I will not be too positive. 285
Homo sum, humani a me nihil alienum puto. As I am a man, I
must be changeable, and sometimes the gravest of us all are
so, even upon ridiculous accidents. Our minds are perpetually wrought on by the temperament of our bodies,
which makes me suspect they are nearer allied than either 290
our philosophers or school divines will allow them to be.
I have observed, says Montaigne, that when the body is
out of order, its companion is seldom at his ease. An ill
dream or a cloudy day has power to change this wretched
creature who is so proud of a reasonable soul, and make him 295
think what he thought not yesterday. And Homer was of this
opinion, as Cicero is pleased to translate him for us:

> *Tales sunt hominum mentes quali pater ipse*
> *Jupiter auctifera lustravit lampade terras.*

Or as the same author, in his *Tusculan Questions*, speaks 300
with more modesty than usual of himself: *nos in diem vivimus;*

280. full] *Q 1-2, 4-6; om. Q 3.*   4-5; by the temperaments *Q 3;*
289. by the temperament] *Q 1-2,*   by temperaments *Q 6.*

286. *Homo . . . puto*] altered from Terence *Heauton-Timorumenos* I. i. 25.
Dryden translates loosely in the next sentence.
292. *Montaigne*] Dryden is probably thinking of *Essays* III. xiii, "Of
Experience": "If my body would govern itself as well, according to my
rule, as my mind does, we should move a little more at our ease" (trans.
Cotton). Similar passages occur toward the end of the same essay.
298-299.] altered from *De fato*, Fragment 3, translating *Odyssey* xviii.
136-137: "The minds of men are like the fruitful light with which father
Jupiter himself has illuminated the earth."
301-302. *nos . . . dicimus*] *Tusculanae disputationes* V. 34: "We live for the
day: whatever strikes our minds as probable, that we say."

quodcunque animos nostros probabilitate percussit, id dicimus. 'Tis
not therefore impossible but that I may alter the conclusion
of my play to restore myself into the good graces of my fair
critics. And your Lordship, who is so well with them, may do 305
me the office of a friend and patron, to intercede with them
on my promise of amendment. The impotent lover in Petron-
ius, though his was a very unpardonable crime, yet was
received to mercy on the terms I offer. *Summa excusationis
meae haec est: placebo tibi, si culpam emendare permiseris.* 310
But I am conscious to myself of offering at a greater
boldness in presenting to your view what my meanness can
produce, than in any other error of my play. And therefore
make haste to break off this tedious address, which has, I
know not how, already run itself into so much of pedantry, 315
with an excuse of Tully's, which he sent with his books *De
finibus* to his friend Brutus: *de ipsis rebus autem, saepenumero
Brute vereor ne reprehendar, cum haec ad te scribam, qui tum in
poesi* (I change it from *philosophia*) *tum in optimo genere poeseos
tantum processeris. Quod si facerem quasi te erudiens, jure reprehen-* 320
*derer. Sed ab eo plurimum absum: nec, ut ea cognoscas quae tibi
notissima sunt ad te mitto: sed quia facillime in nomine tuo
acquiesco, & quia te habeo aequissimum eorum studiorum, quae
mihi communia tecum sunt, aestimatorem & judicem.* Which you
may please, my Lord, to apply to yourself, from him who is 325
Your Lordship's most obedient humble servant,

DRYDEN

307. impotent] *Q 1-2, 4-6*; impor-   327. DRYDEN] *Q 1-5*; John Dryden
tant *Q 3*.   *Q 6*.

309-310. *Summa . . . permiseris*] from the letter of Polyaenus to Circe,
Satyricon 130: "The sum of my plea is this: I shall please you if you will
permit me to amend my fault."
317-324. *de ipsis . . . judicem*] Cicero *De finibus* III. ii. 6, trans. Harris
Rackham (Loeb Classics [New York, 1914], pp. 221, 223): "As regards
my subject, I often fear, Brutus, that I shall meet with censure for writing
upon this topic to you, who are yourself so great an adept in [poetry], and
in the highest branch of [poetry]. Did I assume the attitude of an instructor,
such censure would be deserved. But nothing could be farther from me. I
dedicate my work to you, not to teach you what you know extremely well
already, but because your name gives me a very comforting sense of sup-
port, and because I find in you a most impartial judge and critic of the
studies which I share with yourself."

PROLOGUE

Our author by experience finds it true,
'Tis much more hard to please himself than you;
And out of no feigned modesty, this day,
Damns his laborious trifle of a play.
Not that it's worse than what before he writ,   5
But he has now another taste of wit;
And, to confess a truth (though out of time),
Grows weary of his long-loved mistress, rhyme.
Passion's too fierce to be in fetters bound,
And nature flies him like enchanted ground.   10
What verse can do, he has performed in this,
Which he presumes the most correct of his;
But spite of all his pride, a secret shame
Invades his breast at Shakespeare's sacred name;
Awed when he hears his godlike Romans rage,   15
He, in a just despair, would quit the stage,
And to an age less polished, more unskilled,
Does with disdain the foremost honors yield.
As with the greater dead he dares not strive,
He would not match his verse with those who live;   20
Let him retire, betwixt two ages cast,
The first of this, and hindmost of the last.
A losing gamester, let him sneak away;
He bears no ready money from the play.
The fate which governs poets thought it fit   25
He should not raise his fortunes by his wit.
The clergy thrive, and the litigious bar;
Dull heroes fatten with the spoils of war;
All southern vices, Heav'n be praised, are here;
But wit's a luxury you think too dear.   30
When you to cultivate the plant are loath,
'Tis a shrewd sign 'twas never of your growth;
And wit in northern climates will not blow,

---

10. *flies*] evades.
27. *bar*] legal profession.
29. *southern vices*] Mediterranean countries, particularly Italy, were thought predisposed to licentiousness by their warm climate.

Except, like orange trees, 'tis housed from snow.
There needs no care to put a playhouse down;   35
'Tis the most desert place of all the town.
We and our neighbors, to speak proudly, are
Like monarchs, ruined with expensive war;
While, like wise English, unconcerned you sit,
And see us play the tragedy of wit.   40

35. put] *Q 1, 3, 5–6*; but *Q 2, 4.*

---

36. *desert*] deserted.
37–38.] an allusion to the rivalry between the King's and the Duke's
companies.

PERSONS REPRESENTED   BY

THE OLD EMPEROR	Mr. Mohun
AURENG-ZEBE, his son	Mr. Hart
MORAT, his younger son	Mr. Kynaston
ARIMANT, Governor of Agra	Mr. Wintershall

DIANET   ⎫   5
SOLYMAN
MIR BABA   ⎬ Indian lords, or Omrahs, of
ABAS   several factions
ASAPH CHAN
FAZEL CHAN ⎭   10

NOURMAHAL, the Empress	Mrs. Marshall
INDAMORA, a captive queen	Mrs. Cox
MELESINDA, wife to Morat	Mrs. Corbett
ZAYDA, favorite slave to the Empress	Mrs. Uphill

Scene: Agra, in the year 1660   15

0.1. PERSONS REPRESENTED   *sonae Q 3, 6.*
... BY] *Q 1–2, 4–5; Dramatis Per-*

---

1. *The Old Emperor*] Shah Jahan, fifth Mogul emperor, reigned from 1628 to 1658, when he was deposed by Aureng-Zebe. Dryden specifies 1660 as the date of his action.

9,10. *Chan*] Khan, in this case a noble.

15. *Agra*] first capital of the Moguls, prominent even after Shah Jahan moved the court to Delhi.

Aureng-Zebe
A Tragedy

ACT I

[*Enter*] Arimant, Asaph Chan, Fazel Chan.

ARIMANT.

Heav'n seems the empire of the east to lay
On the success of this important day;
Their arms are to the last decision bent,
And fortune labors with the vast event.
She now has in her hand the greatest stake   5
Which for contending monarchs she can make.
Whate'er can urge ambitious youth to fight
She pompously displays before their sight;
Laws, empire, all permitted to the sword,
And fate could ne'er an ampler scene afford.   10

ASAPH.

Four several armies to the field are led,
Which, high in equal hopes, four princes head.
Indus and Ganges, our wide empire's bounds,
Swell their dyed currents with their natives' wounds;
Each purple river winding, as he runs,   15
His bloody arms about his slaughtered sons.

FAZEL.

I well remember you foretold the storm
When first the brothers did their factions form;
When each, by cursed cabals of women, strove
To draw th'indulgent king to partial love.   20

ARIMANT.

What Heav'n decrees, no prudence can prevent.

---

1. *empire of the east*] the Mogul Empire in India.
19. *cabals*] conspiracies.

To cure their mad ambition they were sent
To rule a distant province, each alone.
What could a careful father more have done?
He made provision against all but fate,   25
While, by his health, we held our peace of state.
The weight of seventy winters pressed him down;
He bent beneath the burthen of a crown.
Sickness, at last, did his spent body seize,
And life almost sunk under the disease;   30
Mortal 'twas thought, at least by them desired,
Who impiously into his years inquired.
As at a signal, straight the sons prepare
For open force, and rush to sudden war;
Meeting, like winds broke loose upon the main,   35
To prove by arms whose fate it was to reign.

ASAPH.

Rebels and parricides!

ARIMANT.

Brand not their actions with so foul a name;
Pity, at least, what we are forced to blame.
When death's cold hand has closed the father's eye,   40
You know the younger sons are doomed to die.
Less ills are chosen greater to avoid,
And nature's laws are by the state's destroyed.
What courage tamely could to death consent,
And not, by striking first, the blow prevent?   45
Who falls in fight cannot himself accuse,
And he dies greatly who a crown pursues.

To them Solyman Agah.

SOLYMAN.

A new express all Agra does affright:
Darah and Aureng-Zebe are joined in fight;
The press of people thickens to the court,   50
Th'impatient crowd devouring the report.

ARIMANT.

T'each changing news they changed affections bring,
And servilely from fate expect a king.

40–41.] i.e., lest they revolt against the successor, a common occurrence.
48. *express*] bulletin.

SOLYMAN.

   The ministers of state, who gave us law,
   In corners, with selected friends, withdraw;   55
   There, in deaf murmurs, solemnly are wise,
   Whisp'ring like winds ere hurricanes arise.
   The most corrupt are most obsequious grown,
   And those they scorned, officiously they own.

ASAPH.

   In change of government   60
   The rabble rule their great oppressors' fate,
   Do sovereign justice, and revenge the state.

SOLYMAN.

   The little courtiers, who ne'er come to know
   The depth of factions, as in mazes go,
   Where int'rests meet and cross so oft, that they   65
   With too much care are wildered in their way.

ARIMANT.

   What of the Emperor?

SOLYMAN.

   Unmoved and brave, he like himself appears,
   And, meriting no ill, no danger fears;
   Yet mourns his former vigor lost so far   70
   To make him now spectator of a war;
   Repining that he must preserve his crown
   By any help or courage but his own;
   Wishes each minute he could unbeget
   Those rebel sons, who dare t'usurp his seat,   75
   To sway his empire with unequal skill,
   And mount a throne which none but he can fill.

ARIMANT.

   Oh had he still that character maintained
   Of valor, which in blooming youth he gained!
   He promised in his east a glorious race;   80
   Now, sunk from his meridian, sets apace.
   But as the sun, when he from noon declines,
   And with abated heat less fiercely shines,
   Seems to grow milder as he goes away,

73. but] *Q 1–5*; but of *Q6*.

---

66. *wildered*] bewildered.

Pleasing himself with the remains of day;   85
So he, who in his youth for glory strove,
Would recompense his age with ease and love.

ASAPH.

The name of father hateful to him grows,
Which for one son produces him three foes.

FAZEL.

Darah, the eldest, bears a generous mind,   90
But to implacable revenge inclined;
Too openly does love and hatred show:
A bounteous master, but a deadly foe.

SOLYMAN.

From Sujah's valor I should much expect,
But he's a bigot of the Persian sect;   95
And by a foreign int'rest seeks to reign,
Hopeless by love the scepter to obtain.

ASAPH.

Morat's too insolent, too much a brave,
His courage to his envy is a slave.
What he attempts, if his endeavors fail   100
T'effect, he is resolved no other shall.

ARIMANT.

But Aureng-Zebe, by no strong passion swayed
Except his love, more temp'rate is, and weighed.
This Atlas must our sinking state uphold;
In council cool, but in performance bold.   105
He sums their virtues in himself alone,
And adds the greatest, of a loyal son;
His father's cause upon his sword he wears,
And with his arms, we hope, his fortune bears.

SOLYMAN.

Two vast rewards may well his courage move: 110
A parent's blessing and a mistress' love.

101. effect] *Q 1–2, 4*; affect *Q 3,
5–6.*

---

95. *Persian sect*] the Chias (or Shiahs), believers in the succession of
Mohammed's son-in-law Aly. The Emperor and the other brothers followed
the Turkish sect, which asserted the claim of Osman.
  98. *brave*] bully, bravo (*OED*, which cites this passage.)

If he succeed, his recompense, we hear,
Must be the captive queen of Cassimere.

To them Abas.

ABAS.

Mischiefs on mischiefs, greater still, and more!
The neighb'ring plain with arms is covered o'er;   115
The vale an iron harvest seems to yield
Of thick-sprung lances in a waving field.
The polished steel gleams terribly from far,
And every moment nearer shows the war.
The horses' neighing by the wind is blown,   120
And castled elephants o'erlook the town.

ARIMANT.

If, as I fear, Morat these pow'rs commands,
Our empire on the brink of ruin stands.
Th'ambitious Empress with her son is joined,
And in his brother's absence has designed   125
The unprovided town to take with ease,
And then the person of the king to seize.

SOLYMAN.

To all his former issue she has shown
Long hate, and labored to advance her own.

ABAS.

These troops are his.   130
Surat he took, and thence, preventing fame,
By quick and painful marches hither came.
Since his approach, he to his mother sent,
And two long hours in close debate were spent.

ARIMANT.

I'll to my charge, the Citadel, repair,   135
And show my duty by my timely care.   [*Exit.*]

---

113. *Cassimere*] Kashmir.
121. *castled*] equipped with structures for defense.
131. *preventing*] anticipating.
135. *Citadel*] the fortress, containing the royal apartments, garrison, audience chambers, etc.

To them the Emperor, *with a letter in his hand. After him an* Ambassador, *with a train following.*

ASAPH.

But see, the Emperor! A fiery red
His brows and glowing temples does o'erspread.
Morat has some displeasing message sent.

AMBASSADOR.

Do not, great sir, misconstrue his intent,   140
Nor call rebellion what was prudent care
To guard himself by necessary war.
While he believed you living, he obeyed;
His governments but as your viceroy swayed.
But when he thought you gone   145
T'augment the number of the blessed above,
He deemed 'em legacies of royal love;
Nor armed his brothers' portions to invade,
But to defend the present you had made.

EMPEROR.

By frequent messages and strict commands   150
He knew my pleasure to discharge his bands.
Proof of my life my royal signet made,
Yet still he armed, came on, and disobeyed.

AMBASSADOR.

He thought the mandate forged, your death concealed,
And but delayed till truth should be revealed.   155

EMPEROR.

News of my death from rumor he received,
And what he wished he easily believed;
But long demurred, though from my hand he knew
I lived, so loath he was to think it true.
Since he pleads ignorance to that command,   160
Now let him show his duty and disband.

AMBASSADOR.

His honor, sir, will suffer in the cause.
He yields his arms unjust if he withdraws,
And begs his loyalty may be declared
By owning those he leads to be your guard.   165

141. Nor] *Q 1*; Not *Q 2–6.*

EMPEROR.

    I in myself have all the guard I need;
    Bid the presumptuous boy draw off with speed.
    If his audacious troops one hour remain,
    My cannon from the fort shall scour the plain.

AMBASSADOR.

    Since you deny him entrance, he demands   170
    His wife, whom cruelly you hold in bands.
    Her, if unjustly you from him detain,
    He justly will by force of arms regain.

EMPEROR.

    O'er him and his a right from Heav'n I have;
    Subject and son, he's doubly born my slave.   175
    But whatsoe'er his own demerits are,
    Tell him I shall not make on women war.
    And yet I'll do her innocence the grace
    To keep her here, as in the safer place.
    But thou who dar'st this bold defiance bring   180
    Mayst feel the rage of an offended king.
    Hence from my sight without the least reply;
    One word, nay one look more, and thou shalt die!

                               Exit Ambassador.

               Re-enter Arimant.

ARIMANT.

    May Heav'n, great monarch, still augment your bliss
    With length of days, and every day like this.   185
    For from the banks of Gemna news is brought
    Your army has a bloody battle fought;
    Darah from loyal Aureng-Zebe is fled,
    And forty thousand of his men lie dead.
    To Sujah next your conquering army drew;   190
    Him they surprised and easily o'erthrew.

EMPEROR.

    'Tis well.

ARIMANT.

    But well! What more could at your wish be done,
    Than two such conquests gained by such a son?

---

186. *Gemna*] Agra is on the Jumna river.

Your pardon, mighty sir,   195
You seem not high enough your joys to rate;
You stand indebted a vast sum to fate,
And should large thanks for the great blessing pay.

EMPEROR.

My fortune owes me greater every day,
And should my joy more high for this appear,   200
It would have argued me before of fear.
How is Heav'n kind, where I have nothing won,
And fortune only pays me with my own?

ARIMANT.

Great Aureng-Zebe did duteous care express,
And durst not push too far his good success;   205
But lest Morat the city should attack,
Commanded his victorious army back.
Which, left to march as swiftly as they may,
Himself comes first, and will be here this day
Before a close-formed seige shut up his way.   210

EMPEROR.

Prevent his purpose! Hence, hence with all thy speed!
Stop him; his entrance to the town forbid.

ARIMANT.

How, sir? Your loyal, your victorious son?

EMPEROR.

Him would I, more than all the rebels, shun.

ARIMANT.

Whom with your pow'r and fortune, sir, you trust,   215
Now to suspect is vain, as 'tis unjust.
He comes not with a train to move your fear,
But trusts himself to be a pris'ner here.
You knew him brave, you know him faithful now;
He aims at fame, but fame from serving you.   220
'Tis said ambition in his breast does rage;
Who would not be the hero of an age?

---

198. great] *Q 1–2*, *4–6*; greatest   199. greater] *Q 1–2*, *4–5*; great
Q 3.   *Q 3, 6.*
                                            210. shut] *Q 1–2*, *4–6*; shuts *Q 3.*

---

201. *before of fear*] afraid before.

All grant him prudent; prudence interest weighs,
And interest bids him seek your love and praise.
I know you grateful: when he marched from hence   225
You bade him hope an ample recompense.
He conquered in that hope, and from your hands
His love, the precious pledge he left, demands.

EMPEROR.

No more! You search too deep my wounded mind,
And show me what I fear, and would not find.   230
My son has all the debts of duty paid;
Our prophet sends him to my present aid.
Such virtue to distrust were base and low;
I'm not ungrateful—or I was not so!
Inquire no farther; stop his coming on;   235
I will not, cannot, dare not see my son.

ARIMANT.

'Tis now too late his entrance to prevent,
Nor must I to your ruin give consent.
At once your people's heart and son's you lose,
And give him all, when you just things refuse.   240

EMPEROR.

Thou lov'st me sure; thy faith has oft been tried
In ten pitched fields, not shrinking from my side;
Yet giv'st me no advice to bring me ease.

ARIMANT.

Can you be cured, and tell not your disease?
I asked you, sir.

EMPEROR.   Thou shouldst have asked again;   245
There hangs a secret shame on guilty men.
Thou shouldst have pulled the secret from my breast,
Torn out the bearded steel to give me rest;
At least thou shouldst have guessed—
Yet thou art honest, thou couldst ne'er have guessed.   250
Hast thou been never base? Did love ne'er bend
Thy frailer virtue to betray thy friend?
Flatter me, make thy court, and say it did;
Kings in a crowd would have their vices hid.

250. ne'er] *Q 2–6*; near *Q 1*.

---

248. *bearded*] barbed.

We would be kept in count'nance, saved from shame,   255
And owned by others who commit the same.
Nay, now I have confessed.
Thou seest me naked and without disguise:
I look on Aureng-Zebe with rival's eyes.
He has abroad my enemies o'ercome,   260
And I have sought to ruin him at home.

ARIMANT.

This free confession shows you long did strive,
And virtue, though oppressed, is still alive.
But what success did your injustice find?

EMPEROR.

What it deserved, and not what I designed.   265
Unmoved she stood, and deaf to all my prayers,
As seas and winds to sinking mariners.
But seas grow calm, and winds are reconciled;
Her tyrant beauty never grows more mild.
Prayers, promises, and threats were all in vain.   270

ARIMANT.

Then cure yourself by generous disdain.

EMPEROR.

Virtue, disdain, despair I oft have tried,
And foiled, have with new arms my foe defied.
This made me with so little joy to hear
The victory, when I the victor fear.   275

ARIMANT.

Something you swiftly must resolve to do,
Lest Aureng-Zebe your secret love should know.
Morat without does for your ruin wait,
And would you lose the buckler of your state?
A jealous Empress lies within your arms,   280
Too haughty to endure neglected charms.
Your son is duteous, but (as man) he's frail,
And just revenge o'er virtue may prevail.

EMPEROR.

Go then to Indamora, say from me,
Two lives depend upon her secrecy.   285

273. defied] *Q 1–2, 4*; defiled *Q 3,
5–6*.

Bid her conceal my passion from my son.
Though Aureng-Zebe return a conqueror,
Both he and she are still within my pow'r.
Say I'm a father, but a lover too;
Much to my son, more to myself, I owe.   290
When she receives him, to her words give law,
And even the kindness of her glances awe.
See, he appears!

> *After a short whisper,* Arimant *departs.*

Enter Aureng-Zebe, *Dianet, and attendants.* Aureng-Zebe *kneels to his father and kisses his hand.*

AURENG-ZEBE.
My vows have been successful as my sword;
My pray'rs are heard: you have your health restored.   295
Once more 'tis given me to behold your face,
The best of kings and fathers to embrace.
Pardon my tears; 'tis joy which bids 'em flow,
A joy which never was sincere till now.
That which my conquest gave I could not prize,   300
Or 'twas imperfect till I saw your eyes.

EMPEROR.
Turn the discourse; I have a reason why
I would not have you speak so tenderly.
Knew you what shame your kind expressions bring,
You would in pity spare a wretched king.   305

AURENG-ZEBE.
A king! You rob me, sir, of half my due;
You have a dearer name, a father too.

EMPEROR.
I had that name.

AURENG-ZEBE.   What have I said or done
That I no longer must be called your son?
'Tis in that name, Heav'n knows, I glory more   310
Than that of prince or that of conqueror.

295. your] *Q 1–5*; you *Q 6*.

299. *sincere*] pure.

−27−

EMPEROR.

> Then you upbraid me; I am pleased to see
> You're not so perfect, but can fail, like me.
> I have no god to deal with.

AURENG-ZEBE.   Now I find
> Some sly court devil has seduced your mind,   315
> Filled it with black suspicions not your own,
> And all my actions through false optics shown.
> I ne'er did crowns ambitiously regard;
> Honor I sought, the generous mind's reward.
> Long may you live! While you the scepter sway   320
> I shall be still most happy to obey.

EMPEROR.

> Oh Aureng-Zebe, thy virtues shine too bright,
> They flash too fierce! I, like the bird of night,
> Shut my dull eyes and sicken at the sight.
> Thou hast deserved more love than I can show,   325
> But 'tis thy fate to give, and mine to owe.
> Thou seest me much distempered in my mind;
> Pulled back, and then pushed forward to be kind.
> Virtue, and—Fain I would my silence break,
> But have not yet the confidence to speak.   330
> Leave me, and to thy needful rest repair.

AURENG-ZEBE.

> Rest is not suiting with a lover's care;
> I have not yet my Indamora seen.

EMPEROR.

> Somewhat I had forgot; come back again.
> So weary of a father's company!   335

AURENG-ZEBE.

> Sir, you were pleased yourself to license me.

EMPEROR.

> You made me no relation of the fight.
> Besides, a rebel's army is in sight.
> Advise me first. Yet go—
> (*Aside.*)   He goes to Indamora; I should take   340

---

330. the] *Q 1-2, 4-5*; this *Q 3, 6.*

336. *license*] allow (to leave).

A kind of envious joy to keep him back,
Yet to detain him makes my love appear.
I hate his presence, and his absence fear.   *Exit.*

AURENG-ZEBE.
To some new clime, or to thy native sky,
Oh friendless and forsaken virtue, fly.   345
Thy Indian air is deadly to thee grown;
Deceit and cankered malice rule thy throne.
Why did my arms in battle prosp'rous prove,
To gain the barren praise of filial love?
The best of kings by women is misled,   350
Charmed by the witchcraft of a second bed.
Against myself I victories have won,
And by my fatal absence am undone.

To him Indamora, *with* Arimant.

But here she comes!
In the calm harbor of whose gentle breast   355
My tempest-beaten soul may safely rest.
Oh my heart's joy! Whate'er my sorrows be,
They cease and vanish in beholding thee!
Care shuns thy walks; as at the cheerful light
The groaning ghosts and birds obscene take flight.   360
By this one view all my past pains are paid,
And all I have to come more easy made.

INDAMORA.
Such sullen planets at my birth did shine,
They threaten every fortune mixed with mine.
Fly the pursuit of my disastrous love,   365
And from unhappy neighborhood remove.

AURENG-ZEBE.
Bid the laborious hind,
Whose hardened hands did long in tillage toil,
Neglect the promised harvest of the soil.
Should I, who cultivated love with blood,   370
Refuse possession of approaching good?

---

367. *hind*] farm laborer.

INDAMORA.

> Love is an airy good opinion makes,
> Which he who only thinks he has, partakes;
> Seen by a strong imagination's beam
> That tricks and dresses up the gaudy dream.　375
> Presented so, with rapture 'tis enjoyed;
> Raised by high fancy, and by low destroyed.

AURENG-ZEBE.

> If love be vision, mine has all the fire
> Which in first dreams young prophets does inspire.
> I dream in you our promised paradise:　380
> An age's tumult of continued bliss.
> But you have still your happiness in doubt,
> Or else 'tis past, and you have dreamt it out.

INDAMORA.

> Perhaps not so.

AURENG-ZEBE.　　Can Indamora prove

> So altered? Is it but "perhaps you love"?　385
> Then farewell all! I thought in you to find
> A balm to cure my much distempered mind.
> I came to grieve a father's heart estranged,
> But little thought to find a mistress changed.
> Nature herself is changed to punish me;　390
> Virtue turned vice, and faith inconstancy.

INDAMORA.

> You heard me not inconstancy confess;
> 'Twas but a friend's advice to love me less.
> Who knows what adverse fortune may befall?
> Arm well your mind; hope little and fear all.　395
> Hope with a goodly prospect feeds your eye,
> Shows, from a rising ground, possession nigh,
> Shortens the distance, or o'erlooks it quite;
> So easy 'tis to travel with the sight.

AURENG-ZEBE.

> Then to despair you would my love betray,　400
> By taking hope, its last kind friend, away.

373. who] *Q 1–2, 4–6; om. Q 3.*   385. you] *Q 1–2, 4–6;* your *Q 3.*

372. *good*] supply "that."   375. *tricks*] disguises, decorates.
381.] the Mohammedan concept of heaven.

You hold the glass, but turn the perspective,
And farther off the lessened object drive.
You bid me fear. In that your change I know;
You would prepare me for the coming blow.   405
But to prevent you, take my last adieu;
I'll sadly tell myself you are untrue
Rather than stay to hear it told by you.   *Going.*

INDAMORA.

Stay, Aureng-Zebe, I must not let you go.
And yet believe yourself your own worst foe;   410
Think I am true, and seek no more to know.
Let in my breast the fatal secret lie;
'Tis a sad riddle, which if known, we die.   *Seeming to pause.*

AURENG-ZEBE.

Fair hypocrite, you seek to cheat in vain;
Your silence argues you ask time to feign.   415
Once more, farewell: the snare in sight is laid;
'Tis my own fault if I am now betrayed.   *Going again.*

INDAMORA.

Yet once more, stay. You shall believe me true,
Though in one fate I wrap myself and you.
Your absence—

ARIMANT.   Hold! You know the hard command   420
I must obey. You only can withstand
Your own mishap. I beg you on my knee,
Be not unhappy by your own decree.

AURENG-ZEBE.

Speak, madam; by (if that be yet an oath)
Your love, I'm pleased we should be ruined both.   425
"Both" is a sound of joy.
In death's dark bow'rs our bridals we will keep,
And his cold hand
Shall draw the curtain when we go to sleep.

INDAMORA.

Know then, that man whom both of us did trust,   430
Has been to you unkind, to me unjust.

402–403.] You turn the telescope around, diminishing rather than
magnifying the image.

The guardian of my faith so false did prove
As to solicit me with lawless love;
Prayed, promised, threatened, all that man could do;
Base as he's great, and need I tell you who?   435

AURENG-ZEBE.
Yes, for I'll not believe my father meant.
Speak quickly, and my impious thoughts prevent.

INDAMORA.
You've said; I wish I could some other name!

ARIMANT.
My duty must excuse me, sir, from blame.
A guard there!

Enter guards.

AURENG-ZEBE.   Slave, for me?

ARIMANT.   My orders are   440
To seize this princess, whom the laws of war
Long since made prisoner.

AURENG-ZEBE.   Villain!

ARIMANT.   Sir, I know
Your birth, nor durst another call me so.

AURENG-ZEBE.
I have redeemed her, and as mine she's free.

ARIMANT.
You may have right to give her liberty,   445
But with your father, sir, that right dispute.
For his commands to me were absolute:
If she disclosed his love, to use the right
Of war, and to secure her from your sight.

AURENG-ZEBE.
I'll rescue her, or die.   *Draws.* 450
And you, my friends, though few, are yet too brave
To see your gen'ral's mistress made a slave.   *All draw.*

INDAMORA.
Hold, my dear love! If so much pow'r there lies
As once you owned, in Indamora's eyes,
Lose not the honor you have early won,   455
But stand the blameless pattern of a son.

452.S.D. *draw*] Q 1–5; *draws* Q 6.

My love your claim inviolate secures;
'Tis writ in fate I can be only yours.
My suff'rings for you make your heart my due;
Be worthy me, as I am worthy you.   460
AURENG-ZEBE (*putting up his sword*).
I've thought, and blessed be you who gave me time;
My virtue was surprised into a crime.
Strong virtue, like strong nature, struggles still,
Exerts itself, and then throws off the ill.
I to a son's and lover's praise aspire,   465
And must fulfill the parts which both require.
How dear the cure of jealousy has cost!
With too much care and tenderness y'are lost.
So the fond youth from hell redeemed his prize,
Till, looking back, she vanished from his eyes!   470
                                              Exeunt severally.

___

469. *youth*] Orpheus.

ACT II

Betwixt the acts a warlike tune is played. Shooting off guns and shouts of soldiers are heard, as in an assault. [*Enter*] Aureng-Zebe, Arimant, Asaph Chan, Fazel Chan, Solyman.

AURENG-ZEBE.

What man could do was by Morat performed;
The fortress thrice himself in person stormed.
Your valor bravely did th'assault sustain,
And filled the moats and ditches with the slain.
Till, mad with rage, into the breach he fired,   5
Slew friends and foes, and in the smoke retired.

ARIMANT.

To us you give what praises are not due;
Morat was thrice repulsed, but thrice by you.
High over all was your great conduct shown;
You sought our safety, but forgot your own.   10

ASAPH.

Their standard, planted on the battlement,
Despair and death among the soldiers sent;
You the bold Omrah tumbled from the wall,
And shouts of victory pursued his fall.

FAZEL.

To you alone we owe this prosp'rous day;   15
Our wives and children rescued from the prey.
Know your own int'rest, sir; where'er you lead
We jointly vow to own no other head.

SOLYMAN.

Your wrongs are known. Impose but your commands;
This hour shall bring you twenty thousand hands.   20

AURENG-ZEBE.

Let them who truly would appear my friends
Employ their swords, like mine, for noble ends.
No more. Remember you have bravely done.
Shall treason end what loyalty begun?
I own no wrong; some grievance I confess,   25
But kings, like gods, at their own time redress.—
(*Aside.*) Yet, some becoming boldness I may use;

10. but] *Q 1–4; 6*; put *Q 5.*

-34-

I've well deserved, nor will he now refuse.
I'll strike my fortunes with him at a heat,
And give him not the leisure to forget.   30

Exit, attended by the Omrahs.

ARIMANT.

Oh Indamora, hide these fatal eyes!
Too deep they wound whom they too soon surprise.
My virtue, prudence, honor, interest, all
Before this universal monarch fall.
Beauty, like ice, our footing does betray;   35
Who can tread sure on the smooth, slippery way?
Pleased with the passage we slide swiftly on,
And see the dangers which we cannot shun.

To him Indamora.

INDAMORA.

I hope my liberty may reach thus far;
These terrace walks within my limits are.   40
I came to seek you, and to let you know
How much I to your generous pity owe.
The King, when he designed you for my guard,
Resolved he would not make my bondage hard.
If otherwise, you have deceived his end,   45
And whom he meant a guardian, made a friend.

ARIMANT.

A guardian's title I must own with shame,
But should be prouder of another name.

INDAMORA.

And therefore 'twas I changed that name before.
I called you friend, and could you wish for more?   50

ARIMANT.

I dare not ask for what you would not grant,
But wishes, madam, are extravagant.
They are not bounded with things possible;
I may wish more than I presume to tell.
Desire's the vast extent of human mind;   55

50. you wish] Q *1-2, 4-6;* wish you
Q *3.*

-35-

It mounts above, and leaves poor hope behind.
I could wish—

INDAMORA.

What?

ARIMANT.

Why did you speak? You've dashed my fancy quite,
Ev'n in th'approaching minute of delight.   60
I must take breath—
Ere I the rapture of my wish renew,
And tell you then it terminates in you.

INDAMORA.

Have you considered what th'event would be?
Or know you, Arimant, yourself or me?   65
Were I no queen, did you my beauty weigh,
My youth in bloom, your age in its decay?

ARIMANT.

I, my own judge, condemned myself before.
For pity, aggravate my crime no more.
So weak I am, I with a frown am slain;   70
You need have used but half so much disdain.

INDAMORA.

I am not cruel yet to that degree;
Have better thoughts, both of yourself and me.
Beauty a monarch is,
Which kingly power magnificently proves   75
By crowds of slaves, and peopled empire loves.
And such a slave as you what queen would lose?
Above the rest I Arimant would choose
For counsel, valor, truth, and kindness too;
All I could wish in man, I find in you.   80

ARIMANT.

What lover could to greater joy be raised!
I am, methinks, a god, by you thus praised.

INDAMORA.

To what may not desert like yours pretend?
You have all qualities—that fit a friend.

76. and] *Q 1–4*, *6*; add *Q 5*.

_____

74–76.] Beauty demonstrates its power by the number of its slaves, and
therefore loves a large empire.

ARIMANT.

So mariners mistake the promised coast,   85
And with full sails on the blind rocks are lost.
Think you my aged veins so faintly beat
They rise no higher than to friendship's heat?
So weak your charms that, like a winter's night
Twinkling with stars, they freeze me while they light?   90

INDAMORA.

Mistake me not, good Arimant; I know
My beauty's pow'r, and what my charms can do.
You your own talent have not learned so well,
But practice one where you can ne'er excel.
You can at most   95
To an indiff'rent lover's praise pretend,
But you would spoil an admirable friend.

ARIMANT.

Never was amity so highly prized,
Nor ever any love so much despised.
Ev'n to myself ridiculous I grow,   100
And would be angry if I knew but how.

INDAMORA.

Do not. Your anger, like your love, is vain:
Whene'er I please, you must be pleased again.
Knowing what pow'r I have your will to bend,
I'll use it, for I need just such a friend.   105
You must perform, not what you think is fit,
But to whatever I propose submit.

ARIMANT.

Madam, you have a strange ascendant gained;
You use me like a courser, spurred and reined.
If I fly out, my fierceness you command,   110
Then soothe and gently stroke me with your hand.
Impose, but use your pow'r of taxing well;
When subjects cannot pay, they soon rebel.

90. Twinkling] *Q 1–2, 4–6*; Twink-   109. reined] *Q 1–2, 4–6*; reigned
ly *Q 3*.   *Q 3*.
92. my charms] *Q 1–2, 4–6*; charms
Q 3.

---

109. *courser*] spirited war horse.

Enter the Emperor, *unseen by them.*

INDAMORA.

My rebel's punishment would easy prove;
You know y'are in my pow'r by making love.   115

ARIMANT.

Would I without dispute your will obey,
And could you in return my life betray?

EMPEROR.

What danger, Arimant, is this you fear?
Or what love-secret which I must not hear?—
(*To her.*)   These altered looks some inward motion show.   120
His cheeks are pale, and yours with blushes glow.

INDAMORA.

'Tis what with justice may my anger move:
He has been bold, and talked to me of love.

ARIMANT (*aside*).

I am betrayed, and shall be doomed to die!

EMPEROR.

Did he, my slave, presume to look so high?   125
That crawling insect, who from mud began,
Warmed by my beams and kindled into man?
Durst he who does but for my pleasure live
Intrench on love, my great prerogative?
Print his base image on his sovereign's coin?   130
'Tis treason if he stamp his love with mine.

ARIMANT.

'Tis true, I have been bold. But if it be
A crime—

INDAMORA.   He means, 'tis only so to me.
You, sir, should praise what I must disapprove.
He insolently talked to me of love,   135
But, sir, 'twas yours; he made it in your name.
You, if you please, may all he said disclaim.

EMPEROR.

I must disclaim whate'er he can express;
His groveling sense will show my passion less.
But stay; if what he said my message be,   140

119. hear] *Q 1–2, 4–6;* here *Q 3.*   131. stamp] *Q 1–2, 4–6;* stampt
                                                        Q 3.

What fear, what danger could arrive from me?
He said he feared you would his life betray.

INDAMORA.

Should he presume again, perhaps I may.
Though in your hands he hazard not his life,
Remember, sir, your fury of a wife,   145
Who, not content to be revenged on you,
The agents of your passion will pursue.

EMPEROR.

If I but hear her named I'm sick that day;
The sound is mortal, and frights life away.
Forgive me, Arimant, my jealous thought;   150
Distrust in lovers is the tender'st fault.
Leave me, and tell thyself in my excuse,
Love and a crown no rivalship can bear,
And precious things are still possessed with fear.
                              Exit Arimant, *bowing.*
This, madam, my excuse to you may plead: 155
Love should forgive the faults which love has made.

INDAMORA.

From me what pardon can you hope to have,
Robbed of my love and treated as a slave?

EMPEROR.

Force is the last relief which lovers find,
And 'tis the best excuse of womankind.   160

INDAMORA.

Force never yet a generous heart did gain;
We yield on parley, but are stormed in vain.
Constraint in all things makes the pleasure less;
Sweet is the love which comes with willingness.

EMPEROR.

No, 'tis resistance that inflames desire,   165
Sharpens the darts of love and blows his fire.
Love is disarmed that meets with too much ease;
He languishes, and does not care to please.

151. tender'st] *Q 1*; tender's *Q 2–6.*

162. *on parley*] to mutual discussion.

And therefore 'tis your golden fruit you guard
With so much care, to make possession hard.   170

INDAMORA.

Was't not enough you took my crown away,
But cruelly you must my love betray?
I was well pleased to have transferred my right,
And better changed your claim of lawless might
By taking him whom you esteemed above   175
Your other sons, and taught me first to love.

EMPEROR.

My son by my command his course must steer;
I bade him love, I bid him now forbear.
If you have any kindness for him still,
Advise him not to shock a father's will.   180

INDAMORA.

Must I advise?
Then let me see him and I'll try t'obey.

EMPEROR.

I had forgot, and dare not trust your way.
But send him word
He has not here an army to command.   185
Remember he and you are in my hand.

INDAMORA.

Yes, in a father's hand whom he has served,
And with the hazard of his life preserved.
But piety to you, unhappy prince,
Becomes a crime, and duty an offense.   190
Against yourself you with your foes combine,
And seem your own destruction to design.

EMPEROR.

You may be pleased your politics to spare;
I'm old enough, and can myself take care.

INDAMORA.

Advice from me was, I confess, too bold;   195
You're old enough—it may be, sir, too old.

---

169. *golden fruit*] like the apples of the Hesperides, guarded by a watchful
dragon.
174. *better . . . might*] changed an illegal claim (by force) to a legal one
(by marriage).

EMPEROR.

You please yourself with your contempt of age,
But love neglected will convert to rage.
If on your head my fury does not turn,
Thank that fond dotage which so much you scorn.   200
But in another's person you may prove
There's warmth for vengeance left, though not for love.

Re-enter Arimant.

ARIMANT.

The Empress has the antechambers passed,
And this way moves with a disordered haste.
Her brows the stormy marks of anger bear.   205

EMPEROR.

Madam, retire; she must not find you here.

                    Exit Indamora *with* Arimant.

Enter Nourmahal *hastily.*

NOURMAHAL.

What have I done that Nourmahal must prove
The scorn and triumph of a rival's love?
My eyes are still the same: each glance, each grace
Keep their first luster and maintain their place,   210
Not second yet to any other face.

EMPEROR.

What rage transports you? Are you well awake?
Such dreams distracted minds in fevers make.

NOURMAHAL.

Those fevers you have giv'n, those dreams have bred
By broken faith and an abandoned bed.   215
Such visions hourly pass before my sight,
Which from my eyes their balmy slumbers fright
In the severest silence of the night;
Visions which in this citadel are seen;
Bright, glorious visions of a rival queen.   220

---

200. *fond*] foolish.
201. *in . . . prove*] i.e., my treatment of Aureng-Zebe may convince you.
207. *prove*] exemplify.

EMPEROR.

    Have patience. My first flames can ne'er decay;
    These are but dreams and soon will pass away.
    Thou knowest my heart, my empire, all is thine;
    In thy own heav'n of love serenely shine,
    Fair as the face of nature did appear   225
    When flowers first peeped and trees did blossoms bear,
    And winter had not yet deformed th'inverted year;
    Calm as the breath which fans our eastern groves,
    And bright as when thy eyes first lighted up our loves.
    Let our eternal peace be sealed by this,   230

                            Offers to kiss her.

    With the first ardor of a nuptial kiss.

NOURMAHAL.

    Me would you have, me your faint kisses prove,
    The dregs and droppings of enervate love?
    Must I your cold long-laboring age sustain,
    And be to empty joys provoked in vain?   235
    Receive you sighing after other charms,
    And take an absent husband in my arms?

EMPEROR.

    Even these reproaches I can bear from you;
    You doubted of my love; believe it true.
    Nothing but love this patience could produce,   240
    And I allow your rage that kind excuse.

NOURMAHAL.

    Call it not patience; 'tis your guilt stands mute;
    You have a cause too foul to bear dispute.
    You wrong me first, and urge my rage to rise,
    Then I must pass for mad; you, meek and wise,   245
    Good man, plead merit by your soft replies.
    Vain privilege poor women have of tongue;
    Men can stand silent and resolve on wrong.

EMPEROR.

    What can I more? My friendship you refuse,
    And even my mildness, as my crime, accuse.   250

228. groves] *Q 1–3*; grove *Q 4–6.*

---

232. *prove*] accept.

NOURMAHAL.

Your sullen silence cheats not me, false man;
I know you think the bloodiest things you can.
Could you accuse me, you would raise your voice,
Watch for my crimes, and in my guilt rejoice.
But my known virtue is from scandal free,   255
And leaves no shadow for your calumny.

EMPEROR.

Such virtue is the plague of human life;
A virtuous woman, but a cursed wife.
In vain of pompous chastity y'are proud;
Virtue's adultery of the tongue, when loud.   260
I with less pain a prostitute could bear
Than the shrill sound of "virtue, virtue" hear.
In unchaste wives
There's yet a kind of recompensing ease:
Vice keeps 'em humble, gives 'em care to please.   265
But against clamorous virtue, what defense?
It stops our mouths and gives your noise pretense.

NOURMAHAL.

Since virtue does your indignation raise,
'Tis pity but you had that wife you praise.
Your own wild appetites are prone to range,   270
And then you tax our humors with your change.

EMPEROR.

What can be sweeter than our native home!
Thither for ease and soft repose we come;
Home is the sacred refuge of our life,
Secured from all approaches but a wife.   275
If thence we fly, the cause admits no doubt:
None but an inmate foe could force us out.
Clamors our privacies uneasy make;
Birds leave their nests disturbed, and beasts their haunts forsake.

NOURMAHAL.

Honor's my crime that has your loathing bred;   280
You take no pleasure in a virtuous bed.

EMPEROR.

What pleasure can there be in that estate

---

251. *cheats*] deceives.

Which your unquietness has made me hate?
I shrink far off,
Dissembling sleep, but wakeful with the fright.   285
The day takes off the pleasure of the night.

NOURMAHAL.

My thoughts no other joys but pow'r pursue,
Or if they did they must be lost in you.
And yet the fault's not mine.
Though youth and beauty cannot warmth command,   290
The sun in vain shines on the barren sand.

EMPEROR.

'Tis true, of marriage bands I'm weary grown.
Love scorns all ties but those that are his own.
Chains that are dragged must needs uneasy prove,
For there's a godlike liberty in love.   295

NOURMAHAL.

What's love to you?
The bloom of beauty other years demands,
Nor will be gathered by such withered hands.
You importune it with a false desire
Which sparkles out and makes no solid fire.   300
This impudence of age, whence can it spring?
All you expect, and yet you nothing bring.
Eager to ask, when you are past a grant;
Nice in providing what you cannot want.
Have conscience; give not her you love this pain;   305
Solicit not yourself and her in vain.
All other debts may compensation find,
But love is strict, and will be paid in kind.

EMPEROR.

Sure, of all ills, domestic are the worst;
When most secure of blessings, we are cursed.   310
When we lay next us what we hold most dear,
Like Hercules, invenomed shirts we wear,

283. me] *Q 1, 3*; we *Q 2, 4–6*.

312. *invenomed shirts*] When Hercules killed Nessus, the dying centaur told the hero's wife to use his blood as a love potion; she dipped a shirt in it, and Hercules subsequently tore his flesh in agony trying to remove the poisoned garment.

And cleaving mischiefs.

NOURMAHAL.   What you merit, have,
And share at least the miseries you gave.
Your days I will alarm, I'll haunt your nights,   315
And worse than age disable your delights.
May your sick fame still languish till it die,
All offices of pow'r neglected lie,
And you grow cheap in every subject's eye.
Then, as the greatest curse that I can give,   320
Unpitied be deposed, and after live.   *Going off.*

EMPEROR.

Stay! And now learn,
How criminal soe'er we husbands are,
'Tis not for wives to push our crimes too far.
Had you still mistress of your temper been,   325
I had been modest and not owned my sin.
Your fury hardens me, and whate'er wrong
You suffer, you have canceled by your tongue.
A guard there! Seize her! She shall know this hour
What is a husband's and a monarch's pow'r.   330
                    Guard seizes her.

Enter Aureng-Zebe.

NOURMAHAL.

I see for whom your charter you maintain;
I must be fettered and my son be slain
That Zelyma's ambitious race may reign.
Not so you promised when my beauty drew
All Asia's vows; when Persia left for you,   335
The realm of Candahar for dow'r I brought,
That long-contended prize for which you fought.

AURENG-ZEBE.

The name of stepmother, your practiced art
By which you have estranged my father's heart,

---

318. *offices*] functions.
333. *Zelyma*] here supposed the mother of Aureng-Zebe.
336. *Candahar*] Kandahar, a city of strategic importance in southern Afghanistan, was conquered several times by both Moguls and Persians. Nourmahal's claim is Dryden's invention.

All you have done against me, or design,   340
Shows your aversion, but begets not mine.
Long may my father India's empire guide,
And may no breach your nuptial vows divide.

EMPEROR.

Since love obliges not, I from this hour
Assume the right of man's despotic pow'r.   345
Man is by nature formed your sex's head,
And is himself the canon of his bed.
In bands of iron fettered you shall be:
An easier yoke than what you put on me.

AURENG-ZEBE (*kneeling*).

Though much I fear my int'rest is not great,   350
Let me your royal clemency intreat.
Secrets of marriage still are sacred held,
Their sweet and bitter by the wise concealed.
Errors of wives reflect on husbands still,
And when divulged proclaim you've chosen ill.   355
And the mysterious pow'r of bed and throne
Should always be maintained, but rarely shown.

EMPEROR.

To so perverse a sex all grace is vain;
It gives 'em courage to offend again.
For with feigned tears they penitence pretend,   360
Again are pardoned, and again offend;
Fathom our pity when they seem to grieve,
Only to try how far we can forgive;
Till, launching out into a sea of strife,
They scorn all pardon and appear all wife.   365
But be it as you please. For your loved sake
This last and fruitless trial I will make.
In all requests your right of merit use,
And know there is but one I can refuse.

He signs to the guards, and they remove from the Empress.

NOURMAHAL.

You've done enough, for you designed my chains;   370

347. canon] *Q 1–2, 4–5*; cannon
Q 3, 6.

---

347. *canon*] law (or lawgiver).

The grace is vanished, but th'affront remains.
Nor is't a grace, or for his merit done;
You durst no farther, for you feared my son.
This you have gained by the rough course you prove:
I'm past repentance, and you past my love.   *Exit.* 375

EMPEROR.

A spirit so untamed the world ne'er bore.

AURENG-ZEBE.

And yet worse usage had incensed her more.
But since by no obligement she is tied,
You must betimes for your defense provide.
I cannot idle in your danger stand,   380
But beg once more I may your arms command.
Two battles your auspicious cause has won;
My sword can perfect what it has begun,
And from your walls dislodge that haughty son.

EMPEROR.

My son, your valor has this day been such   385
None can enough admire or praise too much.
But now, with reason, your success I doubt;
Her faction's strong within, his arms without.

AURENG-ZEBE.

I left the city in a panic fright;
Lions they are in council, lambs in fight.   390
But my own troops, by Mirzah led, are near:
I by tomorrow's dawn expect 'em here.
To favor 'em, I'll sally out ere day,
And through our slaughtered foes enlarge their way.

EMPEROR.

Age has not yet   395
So shrunk my sinews or so chilled my veins,
But conscious virtue in my breast remains.
But had I now
That strength with which my boiling youth was fraught
When in the vale of Balasor I fought,   400

---

374. *prove*] undertake.
400. *Balasor*] district and capital in the state of Orissa, southwest of Calcutta.

And from Bengal their captive monarch brought;
When elephant 'gainst elephant did rear
His trunk, and castles justled in the air;
My sword thy way to victory had shown,
And owed the conquest to itself alone.   405

AURENG-ZEBE.

Those fair ideas to my aid I'll call,
And emulate my great original.
Or, if they fail, I will invoke in arms
The pow'r of love, and Indamora's charms.

EMPEROR.

I doubt the happy influence of your star;   410
T'invoke a captive's name bodes ill in war.

AURENG-ZEBE.

Sir, give me leave to say, whatever now
The omen prove, it boded well to you.
Your royal promise, when I went to fight,
Obliged me to resign a victor's right.   415
Her liberty I fought for and I won,
And claim it as your general and your son.

EMPEROR.

My ears still ring with noise; I'm vexed to death,
Tongue-killed, and have not yet recovered breath.
Nor will I be prescribed my time by you;   420
First end the war, and then your claim renew.
While to your conduct I my fortune trust,
To keep this pledge of duty is but just.

AURENG-ZEBE.

Some hidden cause your jealousy does move,
Or you would ne'er suspect my loyal love.   425

EMPEROR.

What love soever by an heir is shown,
He waits but time to step into the throne.
You're neither justified nor yet accused;
Meanwhile, the pris'ner with respect is used.

428. nor] *Q 1–5*; not *Q 6*.

401. *Bengal*] province in northeast India, including the delta of the
Ganges.

AURENG-ZEBE.

 I know the kindness of her guardian such,   430
 I need not fear too little, but too much.
 But how, sir, how have you from virtue swerved,
 Or what so ill return have I deserved?
 You doubt not me, nor have I spent my blood
 To have my faith no better understood.   435
 Your soul's above the baseness of distrust;
 Nothing but love could make you so unjust.

EMPEROR.

 You know your rival, then; and know 'tis fit
 The son's should to the father's claim submit.

AURENG-ZEBE.

 Sons may have right which they can never quit.   440
 Yourself first made that title which I claim,
 First bid me love, and authorized my flame.

EMPEROR.

 The value of my gift I did not know;
 If I could give, I can resume it too.

AURENG-ZEBE.

 Recall your gift, for I your power confess;   445
 But first take back my life, a gift that's less.
 Long life would now but a long burthen prove;
 You're grown unkind, and I have lost your love.
 My grief let unbecoming speeches fall;
 I should have died, and not complained at all.   450

EMPEROR.

 Witness, ye pow'rs,
 How much I suffered and how long I strove
 Against th'assaults of this imperious love!
 I represented to myself the shame
 Of perjured faith and violated fame,   455
 Your great deserts, how ill they were repayed;
 All arguments in vain I urged and weighed;
 For mighty love, who prudence does despise,
 For reason showed me Indamora's eyes.
 What would you more? My crime I sadly view,   460
 Acknowledge, am ashamed, and yet pursue.

439. son's] *Q 1–5*; sons *Q 6.*

AURENG-ZEBE.

Since you can love, and yet your error see,
The same resistless pow'r may plead for me.
With no less ardor I my claim pursue;
I love, and cannot yield her even to you.   465

EMPEROR.

Your elder brothers, though o'ercome, have right;
The youngest yet in arms prepared to fight.
But, yielding her, I firmly have decreed
That you alone to empire shall succeed.

AURENG-ZEBE

To after ages let me stand a shame   470
When I exchange for crowns my love or fame.
You might have found a mercenary son
To profit of the battles he had won.
Had I been such, what hindered me to take
The crown? Nor had th' exchange been yours to make.   475
While you are living I no right pretend;
Wear it, and let it where you please descend.
But from my love 'tis sacrilege to part;
There, there's my throne, in Indamora's heart.

EMPEROR.

'Tis in her heart alone that you must reign;   480
You'll find her person difficult to gain.
Give willingly what I can take by force,
And know obedience is your safest course.

AURENG-ZEBE.

I'm taught by honor's precepts to obey;
Fear to obedience is a slavish way.   485
If aught my want of duty could beget,
You take the most prevailing means—to threat.
Pardon your blood that boils within my veins;
It rises high, and menacing disdains.
Even death's become to me no dreadful name;   490
I've often met him, and have made him tame.
In fighting fields, where our acquaintance grew,
I saw him and condemned him first for you.

---

476. you] *Q 1-2, 4-6*; your *Q 3*.

468. *yielding her*] if you yield her.

EMPEROR.

    Of formal duty make no more thy boast;
    Thou disobey'st where it concerns me most.   495
    Fool, with both hands thus to push back a crown,
    And headlong cast thyself from empire down!
    Though Nourmahal I hate, her son shall reign;
    Inglorious thou by thy own fault remain.
    Thy younger brother I'll admit this hour;   500
    So mine shall be thy mistress, his thy pow'r.   *Exit.*

AURENG-ZEBE.

    How vain is virtue which directs our ways
    Through certain danger to uncertain praise!
    Barren and airy name! Thee fortune flies,
    With thy lean train, the pious and the wise.   505
    Heav'n takes thee at thy word, without regard,
    And lets thee poorly be thy own reward.
    The world is made for the bold impious man,
    Who stops at nothing, seizes all he can.
    Justice to merit does weak aid afford;   510
    She trusts her balance, and neglects her sword.
    Virtue is nice to take what's not her own,
    And while she long consults, the prize is gone.

To him Dianet.

DIANET.

    Forgive the bearer of unhappy news;
    Your altered father openly pursues   515
    Your ruin, and to compass his intent,
    For violent Morat in haste has sent.
    The gates he ordered all to be unbarred,
    And from the marketplace to draw the guard.

AURENG-ZEBE.

    How look the people in this turn of state?   520

DIANET.

    They mourn your ruin as their proper fate,

503. danger] *Q 1-2, 4-6*; dangers   510. weak] *Q 1-2, 4-6*; week *Q 3.*
Q 3.

    511.] alluding to the two emblems of the figure of Justice: scales and
sword.
    512. *nice to take*] scrupulous about taking.

Cursing the Empress, for they think it done
By her procurement to advance her son.
Him too, though awed, they scarcely can forbear;
His pride they hate, his violence they fear.   525
All bent to rise, would you appear their chief,
Till your own troops come up to your relief.

AURENG-ZEBE.

Ill-treated and forsaken as I am,
I'll not betray the glory of my name.
'Tis not for me, who have preserved a state,   530
To buy an empire at so base a rate.

DIANET.

The points of honor poets may produce:
Trappings of life, for ornament, not use.
Honor which only does the name advance
Is the mere raving madness of romance.   535
Pleased with a word, you may sit tamely down
And see your younger brother force the crown.

AURENG-ZEBE.

I know my fortune in extremes does lie:
The sons of Indostan must reign or die;
That desperate hazard courage does create,   540
As he plays frankly who has least estate;
And that the world the coward will despise,
When life's a blank, who pulls not for a prize.

DIANET.

Of all your knowledge this vain fruit you have,
To walk with eyes broad open to your grave.   545

---

524. *forbear*] endure.

532.] Poets may debate the niceties of the code of honor.

539. *Indostan*] Hindustan, here apparently applied to the Mogul empire generally (Beaurline-Bowers).

541. *plays frankly*] gambles freely.

542. *that*] either "as" (paralleling the *As* in l. 541), or loosely governed by the *I know* in l. 538. The sense of ll. 540–543 is "My plight requires the raw courage of the gambler who must stake his last cent and his reputation on the chance of drawing the winning card."

543. *pulls*] takes a card.

AURENG-ZEBE.

From what I've said conclude without reply,
I neither would usurp nor tamely die.
Th'attempt to fly would guilt betray, or fear;
Besides, 'twere vain: the fort's our prison here.
Somewhat I have resolved—   550
Morat, perhaps, has honor in his breast,
And in extremes bold counsels are the best.
Like emp'ric remedies they last are tried,
And by th'event condemned or justified.
Presence of mind and courage in distress   555
Are more than armies to procure success.   *Exeunt.*

546. conclude] *Q 1–4;* concluded   *Q 6 (i.e., Q 3 and Q 6 take the first*
Q 5–6.   *word in the line as a S.P.).*
551. Morat, perhaps] *Q 1–2, 4–5;*   556. *Exeunt] Exit Q 1–6.*
DIA. Perhaps *Q 3;* MOR. perhaps

553. *emp'ric]* quack.

ACT III

[Enter] Arimant, *with a letter in his hand*; Indamora.

ARIMANT.

 And I the messenger to him from you?
 Your empire you to tyranny pursue;
 You lay commands both cruel and unjust,
 To serve my rival and betray my trust.

INDAMORA.

 You first betrayed your trust in loving me,   5
 And should I not my own advantage see?
 Serving my love you may my friendship gain;
 You know the rest of your pretenses vain.
 You must, my Arimant, you must be kind;
 'Tis in your nature, and your noble mind.   10

ARIMANT.

 I'll to the king, and straight my trust resign.

INDAMORA.

 His trust you may, but you shall never mine.
 Heav'n made you love me for no other end
 But to become my confidant and friend.
 As such, I keep no secret from your sight,   15
 And therefore make you judge how ill I write;
 Read it and tell me freely then your mind,
 If 'tis indited, as I meant it, kind.

ARIMANT *(reading)*.

 "I ask not Heav'n my freedom to restore,
 But only for your sake"—I'll read no more.   20
 And yet I must.—
 (Reading.) "Less for my own than for your sorrow sad"—
 Another line like this would make me mad!—
 (As reading.) Heav'n! She goes on! Yet more, and yet more
                kind!

 Each sentence is a dagger to my mind.—   25
 (Reading.) "See me this night;
 Thank fortune, who did such a friend provide,

8. rest] *Q 1*; best *Q 2–6.*   23. mad] *Q 1–5*; made *Q 6.*
13. me for] *Q 1–2, 4–6*; for me
Q 3.

For faithful Arimant shall be your guide."
Not only to be made an instrument,
But pre-engaged without my own consent!   30

INDAMORA.

Unknown t'engage you still augments my score,
And gives you scope of meriting the more.

ARIMANT.

The best of men
Some int'rest in their actions must confess;
None merit but in hope they may possess.   35
The fatal paper rather let me tear
Than, like Bellerophon, my own sentence bear.

INDAMORA.

You may, but 'twill not be your best advice;
'Twill only give me pains of writing twice.
You know you must obey me soon or late;   40
Why should you vainly struggle with your fate?

ARIMANT.

I thank thee, Heav'n; thou hast been wondrous kind!
Why am I thus to slavery designed,
And yet am cheated with a free-born mind?
Or make thy orders with my reason suit,   45
Or let me live by sense, a glorious brute.   *She frowns.*
You frown, and I obey with speed, before
That dreadful sentence comes, "See me no more."
"See me no more!" That sound, methinks, I hear
Like the last trumpet thund'ring in my ear.   50

Enter Solyman.

SOLYMAN.

The princess Melesinda, bathed in tears,
And tossed alternately with hopes and fears,
If your affairs such leisure can afford,
Would learn from you the fortunes of her lord.

31. augments] *Q 1–2, 4;* augment
Q 3, 5–6.

---

31. *still . . . score*] gives me more points.
37. *Bellerophon*] Proteus gave Bellerophon a letter recommending him
to Iobates, but adding a request that he be killed.
45–46. *Or . . . or*] either . . . or.

ARIMANT.

Tell her that I some certainty may bring;   55
I go this minute to attend the king.

INDAMORA.

This lonely turtle I desire to see;
Grief, though not cured, is eased by company.

ARIMANT (*to* Solyman).

Say if she please she hither may repair,
And breathe the freshness of the open air.   60

Exit Solyman.

INDAMORA.

Poor princess! How I pity her estate,
Wrapped in the ruins of her husband's fate!
She mourned Morat should in rebellion rise,
Yet he offends and she's the sacrifice.

ARIMANT.

Not knowing his design, at court she stayed,   65
Till by command close pris'ner she was made.
Since when,
Her chains with Roman constancy she bore,
But that, perhaps, an Indian wife's is more.

INDAMORA.

Go, bring her comfort; leave me here alone.   70

ARIMANT.

My love must still be in obedience shown.

Exit Arimant.

Enter Melesinda, *led by* Solyman, *who retires afterwards.*

INDAMORA.

When graceful sorrow in her pomp appears,
Sure she is dressed in Melesinda's tears.
Your head reclined (as hiding grief from view)
Droops like a rose surcharged with morning dew.   75

MELESINDA.

Can flow'rs but droop in absence of the sun
Which waked their sweets? And mine, alas, is gone.

66. by] *Q 1–4*; my *Q 5–6.*

57. *turtle*] turtle dove.

–56–

But you the noblest charity express,
For they who shine in courts still shun distress.

INDAMORA.

    Distressed myself, like you, confined I live,   80
And therefore can compassion take, and give.
We're both love's captives, but with fate so cross,
One must be happy by the other's loss;
Morat or Aureng-Zebe must fall this day.

MELESINDA.

    Too truly Tamerlane's successors they;   85
Each thinks a world too little for his sway.
Could you and I the same pretenses bring,
Mankind should with more ease receive a king.
I would to you the narrow world resign,
And want no empire while Morat was mine.   90

INDAMORA.

    Wished freedom I presage you soon will find,
If Heav'n be just and be to virtue kind.

MELESINDA.

    Quite otherwise my mind foretells my fate:
Short is my life, and that unfortunate.
Yet should I not complain, would Heav'n afford   95
Some little time ere death to see my lord.

INDAMORA.

    These thoughts are but your melancholy's food,
Raised from a lonely life and dark abode.
But whatsoe'er our jarring fortunes prove,
Though our lords hate, methinks we two may love.   100

MELESINDA.

    Such be our loves as may not yield to fate;
I bring a heart more true than fortunate.

Giving their hands.

To them Arimant.

ARIMANT.

    I come with haste surprising news to bring:
In two hours time since last I saw the king,

96. ere] *Q 1–2*; e're *Q 3–5*; e'er *Q 6*.

---

85. *Tamerlane*] The Mongol conqueror (d. 1405) was a common emblem
of pride.

Th'affairs of court have wholly changed their face.   105
Unhappy Aureng-Zebe is in disgrace,
And your Morat (proclaimed the successor)
Is called to awe the city with his power.
Those trumpets his triumphant entry tell,
And now the shouts waft near the Citadel.   110

INDAMORA [*to* Melesinda].
See, madam, see th'event by me foreshown;
I envy not your chance, but grieve my own.

MELESINDA.
A change so unexpected must surprise,
And more, because I am unused to joys.

INDAMORA.
May all your wishes ever prosp'rous be,   115
But I'm too much concerned th'event to see.
My eyes too tender are
To view my lord become the public scorn.
I came to comfort, and I go to mourn.

                                              Taking her leave.

MELESINDA.
Stay; I'll not see my lord   120
Before I give your sorrow some relief,
And pay the charity you lent my grief.
Here he shall see me first, with you confined;
And if your virtue fail to move his mind,
I'll use my int'rest that he may be kind.   125
Fear not; I never moved him yet in vain.

INDAMORA.
So fair a pleader any cause may gain.

MELESINDA.
I have no taste, methinks, of coming joy,
For black presages all my hopes destroy.
"Die," something whispers, "Melesinda, die;   130
Fulfil, fulfil thy mournful destiny."
Mine is a gleam of bliss too hot to last;
Wat'ry it shines, and will be soon o'ercast.

---

133. *Wat'ry it shines*] i.e., like a star or planet which portends rain.

Indamora *and* Melesinda *re-enter, as into the chamber.*

ARIMANT.

Fortune seems weary grown of Aureng-Zebe,
While to her new-made favorite, Morat,   135
Her lavish hand is wastefully profuse:
With fame and flowing honors tided in,
Borne on a swelling current smooth beneath him;
The king and haughty Empress, to our wonder,
If not attoned, yet seemingly at peace,   140
As fate for him that miracle reserved.

Enter in triumph Emperor, Morat, *and train.*

EMPEROR.

I have confessed I love.
As I interpret fairly your design,
So look not with severer eyes on mine.
Your fate has called you to th'imperial seat;   145
In duty be, as you in arms are, great.
For Aureng-Zebe a hated name is grown,
And love less bears a rival than the throne.

MORAT.

To me the cries of fighting fields are charms;
Keen be my sable, and of proof my arms.   150
I ask no other blessing of my stars,
No other prize but fame, nor mistress but the wars.
I scarce am pleased I tamely mount the throne.
Would Aureng-Zebe had all their souls in one;
With all my elder brothers I would fight,   155
And so from partial nature force my right.

EMPEROR.

Had we but lasting youth and time to spare,
Some might be thrown away on fame and war.
But youth, the perishing good, runs on too fast,
And, unenjoyed, will spend itself to waste;   160
Few know the use of life before 'tis past.

---

136. lavish] *Q 1–2, 4–6;* lavisht *Q 3.*   150. be] *Q 1–2, 4;* by *Q 3, 5–6.*
140. attoned] *Q 1, 3–6;* atoned *Q 2.*   159. good] *Q 1–2, 4–5;* goods *Q 3, 6*

140. *attoned*] in harmony.
150. *sable*] saber.

Had I once more thy vigor to command,
I would not let it die upon my hand.
No hour of pleasure should pass empty by;
Youth should watch joys, and shoot 'em as they fly.   165

MORAT.

Methinks all pleasure is in greatness found.
Kings, like Heav'n's eye, should spread their beams around,
Pleased to be seen while glory's race they run;
Rest is not for the chariot of the sun.
Subjects are stiff-necked animals; they soon   170
Feel slackened reins, and pitch their rider down.

EMPEROR.

To thee that drudgery of pow'r I give:
Cares be thy lot. Reign thou, and let me live.
The fort I'll keep for my security,
Bus'ness and public state resign to thee.   175

MORAT.

Luxurious kings are to their people lost;
They live like drones upon the public cost.
My arms from pole to pole the world shall shake,
And, with myself, keep all mankind awake.

EMPEROR.

Believe me, son, and needless trouble spare: 180
'Tis a base world, and is not worth our care.
The vulgar, a scarce animated clod,
Ne'er pleased with aught above 'em, prince or God.
Were I a god the drunken globe should roll;
The little emmets with the human soul   185
Care for themselves, while at my ease I sat,
And second causes did the work of fate.
Or, if I did take care, that care should be
For wit that scorned the world and lived like me.

183. above 'em,] above 'em Q 3;   'em, above Q 1-2, 4-5; 'em above
                                   Q 6.

183. *Ne'er*] supply "are."
185. *emmets*] ants.
187. *second*] natural (as opposed to divine).

To them Nourmahal, Zayda, *and attendants.*

NOURMAHAL (*embracing her son*).
    My dear Morat,   190
    This day propitious to us all has been;
    You're now a monarch's heir, and I a queen.
    Your youthful father now may quit the state,
    And finds the ease he sought indulged by fate.
    Cares shall not keep him on the throne awake,   195
    Nor break the golden slumbers he would take.

EMPEROR.
    In vain I struggled to the goal of life
    While rebel sons and an imperious wife
    Still dragged me backward into noise and strife.

MORAT.
    Be that remembrance lost, and be't my pride   200
    To be your pledge of peace on either side.

To them Aureng-Zebe.

AURENG-ZEBE.
    With all th'assurance innocence can bring,
    Fearless without because secure within,
    Armed with my courage, unconcerned I see
    This pomp; a shame to you, a pride to me.   205
    Shame is but where with wickedness 'tis joined,
    And while no baseness in this breast I find,
    I have not lost the birthright of my mind.

EMPEROR.
    Children (the blind effect of love and chance,
    Formed by their sportive parents' ignorance)   210
    Bear from their birth th'impressions of a slave,
    Whom Heav'n for play-games first, and then for service gave.
    One then may be displaced, and one may reign,
    And want of merit render birthright vain.

MORAT.
    Comes he t'upbraid us with his innocence?   215
    Seize him, and take the preaching Brachman hence.

---

193. *youthful*] intended ironically.
216. *Brachman*] Brahmin; derogatory from a Moslem (Beaurline-Bowers).

AURENG-ZEBE (*to his father*).

>   Stay, sir. I from my years no merit plead;
>   All my designs and acts to duty lead.
>   Your life and glory are my only end,
>   And for that prize I with Morat contend.   220

MORAT.

>   Not him alone; I all mankind defy.
>   Who dares adventure more for both than I?

AURENG-ZEBE.

>   I know you brave, and take you at your word;
>   That present service which you vaunt, afford.
>   Our two rebellious brothers are not dead;   225
>   Though vanquished, yet again they gather head.
>   I dare you as your rival in renown,
>   March out your army from th'imperial town;
>   Choose whom you please, the other leave to me,
>   And set our father absolutely free.   230
>   This if you do, to end all future strife
>   I am content to lead a private life,
>   Disband my army to secure the state,
>   Nor aim at more, but leave the rest to fate.

MORAT.

>   I'll do't! Draw out my army on the plain.   235
>   War is to me a pastime, peace a pain.

EMPEROR (*to* Morat).

>   Think better first.—
>   (*To* Aureng-Zebe.)   You see yourself enclosed beyond escape,
>   And therefore, Proteus-like, you change your shape.
>   Of promise prodigal while pow'r you want,   240
>   And preaching in the self-denying cant.

MORAT.

>   Plot better, for these arts too obvious are
>   Of gaining time, the masterpiece of war.
>   Is Aureng-Zebe so known?

AURENG-ZEBE.   If acts like mine,

>   So far from int'rest, profit, or design,   245
>   Can show my heart, by those I would be known.

---

232. life] *Q 1–5; om. Q 6.*

---

239. *Proteus*] mythological character who could change shape at will.

I wish you could as well defend your own.
My absent army for my father fought;
Yours in these walls is to enslave him brought.
If I come singly, you an armed guest,   250
The world with ease may judge whose cause is best.

MORAT.

My father saw you ill designs pursue,
And my admission showed his fear of you.

AURENG-ZEBE.

Himself best knows why he his love withdraws;
I owe him more than to declare the cause.   255
But still I press our duty may be shown
By arms.

MORAT.   I'll vanquish all his foes alone.

AURENG-ZEBE.

You speak as if you could the fates command,
And had no need of any other hand.
But since my honor you so far suspect,   260
'Tis just I should on your designs reflect.
To prove yourself a loyal son, declare
You'll lay down arms when you conclude the war.

MORAT.

No present answer your demand requires;
The war once done, I'll do what Heav'n inspires.   265
And while the sword this monarchy secures,
'Tis managed by an abler hand than yours.

EMPEROR (*apart*).

Morat's design a doubtful meaning bears.
In Aureng-Zebe true loyalty appears;
He for my safety does his own despise.   270
Still with his wrongs I find his duty rise.
I feel my virtue struggling in my soul,
But stronger passion does its pow'r control.—
(*To* Aureng-Zebe *apart*.)   Yet be advised your ruin to prevent.
You might be safe if you would give consent.   275

AURENG-ZEBE [*aside to* Emperor].

So to your welfare I of use may be,

271. wrongs] *Q 1–2, 4–6;* wrong
Q 3.

256. *press*] insist.

My life or death are equal both to me.
EMPEROR [*aside to* Aureng-Zebe].
The people's hearts are yours, the fort yet mine.
Be wise, and Indamora's love resign.
I am observed; remember that I give   280
This my last proof of kindness: die, or live.
AURENG-ZEBE [*aside to* Emperor].
Life with my Indamora I would choose,
But losing her, the end of living lose.
I had considered all I ought before,
And fear of death can make me change no more.   285
The people's love so little I esteem,
Condemned by you I would not live by them.
May he who must your favor now possess,
Much better serve you, and not love you less.
EMPEROR (*aloud*).
I've heard you; and, to finish the debate,   290
Commit that rebel pris'ner to the state!
MORAT.
The deadly draught he shall begin this day,
And languish with insensible decay.
AURENG-ZEBE.
I hate the ling'ring summons to attend;
Death all at once would be the nobler end.   295
Fate is unkind! Methinks a general
Should warm, and at the head of armies, fall.—
(*To his father.*)   And my ambition did that hope pursue,
That so I might have died in fight for you.
MORAT.
Would I had been disposer of thy stars;   300
Thou shouldst have had thy wish, and died in wars.
'Tis I, not thou, have reason to repine
That thou shouldst fall by any hand but mine.
AURENG-ZEBE.
When thou wert formed, Heav'n did a man begin,
But the brute soul, by chance, was shuffled in.   305
In woods and wilds thy monarchy maintain,
Where valiant beasts by force and rapine reign.

277. or] *Q 1–2*; and *Q 3–6*.

In life's next scene, if transmigration be,
Some bear or lion is reserved for thee.

MORAT.

Take heed thou com'st not in that lion's way.   310
I prophesy thou wilt thy soul convey
Into a lamb, and be again my prey.
Hence with that dreaming priest!

NOURMAHAL.   Let me prepare
The pois'nous draught; his death shall be my care.
Near my apartment let him pris'ner be,   315
That I his hourly ebbs of life may see.

AURENG-ZEBE.

My life I would not ransom with a pray'r;
'Tis vile, since 'tis not worth my father's care.—
[*To his father.*]   I go not, sir, indebted to my grave:
You paid yourself, and took the life you gave.   *Exit.* 320

EMPEROR (*aside*).

Oh that I had more sense of virtue left,
Or were of that which yet remains bereft!
I've just enough to know how I offend,
And to my shame have not enough to mend.—
Lead to the Mosque.   325

MORAT.

Love's pleasures why should dull devotion stay?
Heav'n to my Melesinda's but the way.
                              Exeunt Emperor, Morat, *and train.*

ZAYDA.

Sure Aureng-Zebe has somewhat of divine,
Whose virtue through so dark a cloud can shine.
Fortune has from Morat this day removed   330
The greatest rival and the best beloved.

NOURMAHAL.

He is not yet removed.

ZAYDA.   He lives, 'tis true,
But soon must die, and what I mourn, by you.

NOURMAHAL (*embracing her eagerly*).

My Zayda, may thy words prophetic be!
I take the omen; let him die by me.   335
He, stifled in my arms, shall lose his breath,
And life itself shall envious be of death.

ZAYDA.

    Bless me. you pow'rs above!

NOURMAHAL.   Why dost thou start?

    Is love so strange, or have I not a heart?
    Could Aureng-Zebe so lovely seem to thee,   340
    And I want eyes that noble worth to see?
    Thy little soul was but to wonder moved;
    My sense of it was higher, and I loved.
    That man, that godlike man, so brave, so great—
    But these are thy small praises I repeat.   345
    I'm carried by a tide of love away;
    He's somewhat more than I myself can say.

ZAYDA.

    Though all th'ideas you can form be true,
    He must not, cannot, be possessed by you.
    If contradicting int'rests could be mixed,   350
    Nature herself has cast a bar betwixt.
    And ere you reach to this incestuous love,
    You must divine and human rights remove.

NOURMAHAL.

    Count this among the wonders love has done;
    I had forgot he was my husband's son!   355

ZAYDA.

    Nay, more; you have forgot who is your own,
    For whom your care so long designed the throne.
    Morat must fall if Aureng-Zebe should rise.

NOURMAHAL.

    'Tis true, but who was ere in love and wise?
    Why was that fatal knot of marriage tied,   360
    Which did, by making us too near, divide?
    Divides me from my sex! For Heav'n, I find,
    Excludes but me alone of womankind.
    I stand with guilt confounded, lost with shame,
    And yet made wretched only by a name.   365
    If names have such command on human life,
    Love's sure a name that's more divine than wife.
    That sovereign power all guilt from action takes—

351. has] *Scott-Saintsbury, Beaurline-*   353. rights] *Q 1-2, 4-6;* rites *Q 3.*
Bowers; hast *Q 1;* hath *Q 2-6.*   368. from] *Q 1-2, 4-6;* of *Q 3.*

At least the stains are beautiful it makes.

ZAYDA.

Th'encroaching ill you early should oppose. 370
Flattered, 'tis worse, and by indulgence grows.

NOURMAHAL.

Alas! And what have I not said or done?
I fought it to the last, and love has won.
A bloody conquest, which destruction brought,
And ruined all the country where he fought. 375
Whether this passion from above was sent
The fate of him Heav'n favors to prevent;
Or as the curse of fortune in excess,
That, stretching, would beyond its reach possess,
And with a taste which plenty does deprave, 380
Loathes lawful good and lawless ill does crave—

ZAYDA.

But yet consider—

NOURMAHAL. No, 'tis loss of time.
Think how to farther, not divert, my crime.
My artful engines instantly I'll move,
And choose the soft and gentlest hour of love. 385
The under-provost of the fort is mine.
But see, Morat! I'll whisper my design.

Enter Morat *with* Arimant, *as talking; attendants.*

ARIMANT.

And for that cause was not in public seen,
But stays in prison with the captive queen.

MORAT.

Let my attendants wait; I'll be alone. 390
Where least of state, there most of love is shown.

NOURMAHAL (*to* Morat).

My son, your bus'ness is not hard to guess:
Long absence makes you eager to possess.

383. not] *Q 1–2, 4–5*; and *Q 3, 6.*   387. I'll] *Q 1–2, 4–5*; I *Q 3, 6.*

384. *engines*] stratagems.
384. *move*] set in motion.

I will not importune you by my stay;
She merits all the love which you can pay.   395

Exit with Zayda.

Re-enter Arimant *with* Melesinda, *then exit.* Morat *runs to* Melesinda
and embraces her.

MORAT.

Should I not chide you, that you chose to stay
In gloomy shades, and lost a glorious day?
Lost the first fruits of joy you should possess
In my return, and made my triumph less?

MELESINDA.

Should I not chide, that you should stay and see   400
Those joys, preferring public pomp to me?
Through my dark cell your shouts of triumph rung;
I heard with pleasure, but I thought 'em long.

MORAT.

The public will in triumphs rudely share,
And kings the rudeness of their joys must bear.   405
But I made haste to set my captive free,
And thought that work was only worthy me.
The fame of ancient matrons you pursue,
And stand a blameless pattern to the new.
I have not words to praise such acts as these,   410
But take my heart and mold it as you please.

MELESINDA.

A trial of your kindness I must make,
Though not for mine so much as virtue's sake.
The Queen of Cassimir—

MORAT.   No more, my love,
That only suit I beg you not to move.   415
That she's in bonds for Aureng-Zebe I know,
And should by my consent continue so;
The good old man, I fear, will pity show.
My father dotes, and let him still dote on;
He buys his mistress dearly with his throne.   420

401. Those] *Q 1–2, 4–6*; These *Q 3.*   404. triumphs] *Q 1–2, 4–6*; triumph
Q 3.

MELESINDA.

See her and then be cruel if you can.

MORAT.

'Tis not with me as with a private man.
Such may be swayed by honor or by love,
But monarchs only by their int'rest move.

MELESINDA.

Heav'n does a tribute for your pow'r demand: 425
He leaves th'oppressed and poor upon your hand.
And those who stewards of his pity prove,
He blesses in return with public love.
In his distress some miracle is shown;
If exiled, Heav'n restores him to his throne.   430
He needs no guard while any subject's near,
Nor like his tyrant neighbors lives in fear.
No plots th'alarm to his retirements give;
'Tis all mankind's concern that he should live.

MORAT.

You promised friendship in your low estate,   435
And should forget it in your better fate;
Such maxims are more plausible than true,
But somewhat must be given to love and you.
I'll view this captive queen, to let her see
Pray'rs and complaints are lost on such as me.   440

MELESINDA.

I'll bear the news. Heav'n knows how much I'm pleased
That by my care th'afflicted may be eased.

As she is going off, enter Indamora.

INDAMORA.

I'll spare your pains and venture out alone,
Since you, fair princess, my protection own.—
                    (*To* Morat, *kneeling, who takes her up.*)
But you, brave prince, a harder task must find;   445
In saving me you would but half be kind.

430. restores] *Q 1–2, 4–6;* restore   446. half] *Q 1–5;* halt *Q 6.*
Q 3.

429. *his*] one who has proven a good steward (l. 427). Dryden changes
referent here.

A humble suppliant at your feet I lie;
You have condemned my better part to die.
Without my Aureng-Zebe I cannot live;
Revoke his doom, or else my sentence give.   450

MELESINDA.

If Melesinda in your love have part
(Which to suspect would break my tender heart),
If love like mine may for a lover plead,
By the chaste pleasures of our nuptial bed,
By all the int'rest my past suff'rings make,   455
And all I yet would suffer for your sake,
By you yourself, the last and dearest tie—

MORAT.

You move in vain, for Aureng-Zebe must die.

INDAMORA.

Could that decree from any brother come?
Nature herself is sentenced in your doom.   460
Piety is no more; she sees her place
Usurped by monsters and a savage race.
From her soft eastern climes you drive her forth
To the cold mansions of the utmost north.
How can our prophet suffer you to reign   465
When he looks down and sees your brother slain?
Avenging furies will your life pursue;
Think there's a Heav'n, Morat, though not for you.

MELESINDA.

Her words imprint a terror on my mind.
What if this death which is for him designed   470
Had been your doom (far be that augury!),
And you, not Aureng-Zebe, condemned to die?
Weigh well the various turns of human fate,
And seek by mercy to secure your state.

INDAMORA.

Had Heav'n the crown for Aureng-Zebe designed,   475
Pity for you had pierced his generous mind.
Pity does with a noble nature suit;
A brother's life had suffered no dispute.

---

452. *suspect*] doubt.

All things have right in life. Our prophet's care
Commands the beings ev'n of brutes to spare.   480
Though int'rest his restraint has justified,
Can life, and to a brother, be denied?

MORAT.

All reasons for his safety urged are weak,
And yet methinks 'tis Heav'n to hear you speak.

MELESINDA.

'Tis part of your own being to invade—   485

MORAT.

Nay, if she fail to move, would you persuade?—

Turning to Indamora.

My brother does a glorious fate pursue,
I envy him that he must fall for you.
He had been base had he released his right;
For such an empire none but kings should fight.   490
If with a father he disputes this prize,
My wonder ceases when I see these eyes.

MELESINDA.

And can you then deny those eyes you praise?
Can beauty wonder, and not pity, raise?

MORAT.

Your intercession now is needless grown,   495
Retire, and let me speak with her alone.—

Melesinda *retires, weeping, to the side of the theater.*

(*Taking Indamora's hand.*)   Queen, that you may not fruitless
tears employ,
I bring you news to fill your heart with joy:
Your lover king of all the east shall reign,
For Aureng-Zebe tomorrow shall be slain.   500

INDAMORA (*starting back*).

The hopes you raised y'ave blasted with a breath;
With triumphs you began, but end with death.
Did you not say my lover should be king?

MORAT.

I, in Morat, the best of lovers bring.
For one forsaken both of earth and Heav'n,   505

---

479. *prophet's*] Mohammed's.

Your kinder stars a nobler choice have given.
My father, while I please, a king appears;
His pow'r is more declining than his years.
An emperor and lover but in show,
But you in me have youth and fortune too.   510
As Heav'n did to your eyes and form divine
Submit the fate of all th'imperial line,
So was it ordered by its wise decree
That you would find 'em all comprised in me.

INDAMORA.

If, sir, I seem not discomposed with rage,   515
Feed not your fancy with a false presage.
Farther to press your courtship is but vain;
A cold refusal carries more disdain.
Unsettled virtue stormy may appear;
Honor like mine serenely is severe.   520
To scorn your person and reject your crown
Disorder not my face into a frown.   *Turns from him.*

MORAT.

Your fortune you should rev'rently have used;
Such offers are not twice to be refused.
I go to Aureng-Zebe, and am in haste   525
For your commands; they're like to be the last.

INDAMORA.

Tell him,
With my own death I would his life redeem,
But less than honor both our lives esteem.

MORAT.

Have you no more?

INDAMORA *(aside).*   What shall I do or say?   530
He must not in this fury go away.—
[*To* Morat.]   Tell him I did in vain his brother move,
And yet he falsely said he was in love.
Falsely, for had he truly loved, at least
He would have giv'n one day to my request.   535

512. the] *Q 1–2, 4–6*; thee *Q 3.*   533. he was] *Q 1–2, 4–6*; we was
529. both] *Q 1–2, 4–6*; doth *Q 3.*   *Q 3.*
530.S.D. *aside*] *Q 1–2*; *om. Q 3–6.*

MORAT [*aside*].

    A little yielding may my love advance.

    She darted from her eyes a sidelong glance

    Just as she spoke, and like her words it flew,

    Seemed not to beg what yet she bid me do.—

    (*To her.*) A brother, madam, cannot give a day;   540

    A servant, and who hopes to merit, may.

MELESINDA (*coming to him*).

    If, sir—

MORAT.

    No more. Set speeches and a formal tale

    With none but statesmen and grave fools prevail.

    Dry up your tears, and practice every grace   545

    That fits the pageant of your royal place.   *Exit.*

MELESINDA (*to* Indamora).

    Madam, the strange reverse of fate you see:

    I pitied you, now you may pity me.   *Exit after him.*

INDAMORA.

    Poor princess! Thy hard fate I could bemoan,

    Had I not nearer sorrows of my own.   550

    Beauty is seldom fortunate when great:

    A vast estate, but overcharged with debt.

    Like those whom want to baseness does betray,

    I'm forced to flatter him I cannot pay.

    Oh would he be content to seize the throne!   555

    I beg the life of Aureng-Zebe alone.

    Whom Heav'n would bless, from pomp it will remove,

    And make their wealth in privacy and love.   *Exit.*

536.S.P.,S.D. MORAT (*aside*)] *Q 1–2*   *l. 537; Q 4–6 omit S.P. and S.D.*
omit S.D.; *Q 3 adds l. 536 to Inda-*   *adding the lines to Indamora's.*
mora's speech but includes S.D. at   539. bid] *Q 1–2, 4–6; did Q 3.*

    541. *servant*] candidate for favor.

ACT IV

Aureng-Zebe *solus.*

[AURENG-ZEBE.]
> Distrust and darkness of a future state
> Make poor mankind so fearful of their fate.
> Death in itself is nothing, but we fear
> To be we know not what, we know not where.   *Soft music.*
> This is the ceremony of my fate: 5
> A parting treat, and I'm to die in state.
> They lodge me as I were the Persian king,
> And with luxurious pomp my death they bring.

                    To him Nourmahal.

NOURMAHAL.
> I thought, before you drew your latest breath,
> To smooth your passage and to soften death;   10
> For I would have you, when you upward move,
> Speak kindly of me to our friends above;
> Nor name me there th'occasion of your fate,
> Or what my interest does, impute to hate.

AURENG-ZEBE.
> I ask not for what end your pomp's designed,   15
> Whether t'insult or to compose my mind;
> I marked it not.
> But knowing death would soon th'assault begin,
> Stood firm collected in my strength within;
> To guard that breach did all my forces guide,   20
> And left unmanned the quiet senses' side.

NOURMAHAL.
> Because Morat from me his being took,
> All I can say will much suspected look.
> 'Tis little to confess your fate I grieve,
> Yet more than you would easily believe.   25

AURENG-ZEBE.
> Since my inevitable death you know,
> You safely unavailing pity show;

0.1. IV] *Q 1–3, 5–6;* VI *Q 4.*

'Tis popular to mourn a dying foe.

NOURMAHAL.

You made my liberty your late request.
Is no return due from a grateful breast?   30
I grow impatient till I find some way
Great offices with greater to repay.

AURENG-ZEBE.

When I consider life, 'tis all a cheat,
Yet, fooled with hope, men favor the deceit,
Trust on, and think tomorrow will repay.   35
Tomorrow's falser than the former day,
Lies worse, and while it says we shall be blest
With some new joys, cuts off what we possessed.
Strange couzenage! None would live past years again,
Yet all hope pleasure in what yet remain;   40
And from the dregs of life think to receive
What the first sprightly running could not give.
I'm tired with waiting for this chemic gold,
Which fools us young and beggars us when old.

NOURMAHAL.

'Tis not for nothing that we life pursue;   45
It pays our hopes with something still that's new:
Each day's a mistress unenjoyed before;
Like travelers, we're pleased with seeing more.
Did you but know what joys your way attend,
You would not hurry to your journey's end.   50

AURENG-ZEBE.

I need not haste the end of life to meet;
The precipice is just beneath my feet.

NOURMAHAL.

Think not my sense of virtue is so small;
I'd rather leap down first and break your fall.
                              Taking him by the hand.
My Aureng-Zebe (may I not call you so?),   55
Behold me now no longer as your foe.

33. consider] *Q 1–2*;   considered   37. Lies] *Q 1–2, 4–6*; Dies *Q 3.*
Q 3–6.   43. gold] *Q 1–2, 4–6*; cold *Q 3.*

39. *couzenage*] deceit.
43. *chemic*] false, counterfeit.

I am not, cannot be your enemy:
Look, is there any malice in my eye?
Pray sit.   *Both sit.*
That distance shows too much respect, or fear;   60
You'll find no danger in approaching near.

AURENG-ZEBE.

Forgive th'amazement of my doubtful state:
This kindness from the mother of Morat!
Or is't some angel, pitying what I bore,
Who takes that shape to make my wonder more?   65

NOURMAHAL.

Think me your better genius in disguise,
Or anything that more may charm your eyes.
Your guardian angel never could excel
In care, nor could he love his charge so well.

AURENG-ZEBE.

Whence can proceed so wonderful a change?   70

NOURMAHAL.

Can kindness to desert like yours be strange?
Kindness by secret sympathy is tied,
For noble souls in nature are allied.
I saw with what a brow you braved your fate,
Yet with what mildness bore your father's hate.   75
My virtue, like a string wound up by art,
To the same sound, when yours was touched, took part;
At distance shook, and trembled at my heart.

AURENG-ZEBE.

I'll not complain my father is unkind
Since so much pity from a foe I find.   80
Just Heav'n reward this act.

NOURMAHAL.

'Tis well the debt no payment does demand;
You turn me over to another hand.
But happy, happy she,
And with the blessed above to be compared,   85

59. sit] *Q 1–2, 4*; sir *Q 3, 5–6*.   75. mildness] *Q 1–2, 4*; boldness
72. tied] *Q 1–2, 4–6*; tried *Q 3*.   *Q 3, 5–6*.
                                                  76. wound] *Q 1–2, 4–6*; would *Q 3*.

76–77. *like . . . part*] an allusion to the sympathetic vibration of tuned
strings.

–76–

Whom you yourself would with yourself reward.
The greatest, nay, the fairest of her kind
Would envy her that bliss which you designed.

AURENG-ZEBE.
    Great princes thus, when favorites they raise,
    To justify their grace, their creatures praise. 90

NOURMAHAL.
    As love the noblest passion we account,
    So to the highest object it should mount.
    It shows you brave when mean desires you shun:
    An eagle only can behold the sun.
    And so must you, if yet presage divine 95
    There be in dreams, or was't a vision mine?

AURENG-ZEBE.
    Of me?

NOURMAHAL. And who could else employ my thought?
    I dreamed your love was by love's goddess sought.
    Officious cupids, hov'ring o'er your head,
    Held myrtle wreaths; beneath your feet were spread 100
    What sweets soe'er Sabean springs disclose,
    Our Indian jasmine, or the Syrian rose.
    The wanton ministers around you strove
    For service, and inspired their mother's love.
    Close by your side, and languishing, she lies, 105
    With blushing cheeks, short breath, and wishing eyes;
    Upon your breast supinely lay her head,
    While on your face her famished sight she fed.
    Then, with a sigh, into these words she broke
    (And gathered humid kisses as she spoke): 110
    "Dull and ingrateful! Must I offer love?
    Desired of gods, and envied ev'n by Jove,
    And dost thou ignorance or fear pretend?
    Mean soul! And dar'st not gloriously offend?"
    Then pressing thus his hand—

AURENG-ZEBE (*rising up*).   I'll hear no more. 115

100. were] *Q 1–2, 4*; was *Q 3, 5–6.*   112. of] *Q 1–2, 4*; by *Q 3, 5–6.*

    98. *love's goddess*] Venus. The Venus-Adonis story was a popular subject
in the arts; Dryden's use of it shows his knowledge of the older typologies.
    101. *Sabean*] belonging to Yemen, a country famous for spices.

'Twas impious to have understood before,
And I, till now, endeavored to mistake
Th'incestuous meaning which too plain you make.

NOURMAHAL.

And why this niceness to that pleasure shown
Where nature sums up all her joys in one;   120
Gives all she can, and laboring still to give,
Makes it so great we can but taste and live;
So fills the senses that the soul seems fled,
And thought itself does for the time lie dead;
Till, like a string screwed up with eager haste,   125
It breaks, and is too exquisite to last?

AURENG-ZEBE.

Heav'ns! Can you this without just vengeance hear?
When will you thunder, if it now be clear?
Yet her alone let not your thunder seize;
I too deserve to die because I please.   130

NOURMAHAL.

Custom our native royalty does awe;
Promiscuous love is nature's general law.
For whosoever the first lovers were,
Brother and sister made the second pair,
And doubled, by their love, their piety.   135

AURENG-ZEBE.

Hence, hence, and to some barbarous climate fly,
Which only brutes in human form does yield,
And man grows wild in nature's common field.
Who eat their parents piety pretend,
Yet there no sons their sacred bed ascend.   140
To veil great sins a greater crime you choose,
And in your incest your adult'ry lose.

NOURMAHAL.

In vain this haughty fury you have shown.
How I adore a soul so like my own!
You must be mine, that you may learn to live;   145
Know joys which only she who loves can give.
Nor think that action you upbraid, so ill:

124. the] *Q 1–2, 4–6;* that *Q 3.*

119. *niceness*] fastidiousness.

I am not changed, I love my husband still;
But love him as he was, when youthful grace
And the first down began to shade his face.   150
That image does my virgin flames renew,
And all your father shines more bright in you.
AURENG-ZEBE.
In me a horror of myself you raise:
Cursed by your love and blasted by your praise.
You find new ways to prosecute my fate,   155
And your least guilty passion was your hate.
NOURMAHAL (*offering him a dagger*).
I beg my death, if you can love deny.
AURENG-ZEBE.
I'll grant you nothing; no, not ev'n to die.
NOURMAHAL (*stamps with her foot*).
Know then, you are not half so kind as I.

Enter mutes, some with swords drawn, one with a cup.

You've chosen, and may now repent too late.   160
Behold th'effect of what you wished—my hate.
                    Taking the cup to present him.
This cup a cure for both our ills has brought;
You need not fear a philtre in the draught.
AURENG-ZEBE (*receiving it from her*).
All must be poison which can come from thee,
But this the least. T'immortal liberty   165
This first I pour, like dying Socrates;
                    Spilling a little of it.
Grim though he be, death pleases when he frees.

As he is going to drink, enter Morat *attended.*

MORAT (*taking the cup from him*).
Make not such haste, you must my leisure stay;
Your fate's deferred, you shall not die today.
NOURMAHAL.
What foolish pity has possessed your mind,   170
To alter what your prudence once designed?

165. least.] Q 1–2; least Q 3–6.
_____

163. *philtre*] love potion.
168. *stay*] await.

MORAT.

> What if I please to lengthen out his date
> A day, and take a pride to cozen fate?

NOURMAHAL.

> 'Twill not be safe to let him live an hour.

MORAT.

> I'll do't to show my arbitrary pow'r.   175

NOURMAHAL.

> Fortune may take him from your hands again,
> And you repent th'occasion lost in vain.

MORAT.

> I smile at what your female fear foresees;
> I'm in fate's place, and dictate her decrees.
> Let Arimant be called.   *Exit one of his attendants.* 180

AURENG-ZEBE.

> Give me the poison and I'll end your strife;
> I hate to keep a poor precarious life.
> Would I my safety on base terms receive,
> Know, sir, I could have lived without your leave.
> But those I could accuse I can forgive;   185
> By my disdainful silence let 'em live.

NOURMAHAL (*to* Morat).

> What am I that you dare to bind my hand?
> So low I've not a murder at command!
> Can you not one poor life to her afford,
> Her who gave up whole nations to your sword?   190
> And from th'abundance of whose soul and heat
> Th'o'erflowing served to make your mind so great?

MORAT.

> What did that greatness in a woman's mind?
> Ill lodged, and weak to act what it designed.
> Pleasure's your portion, and your slothful ease;   195
> When man's at leisure, study how to please,
> Soften his angry hours with servile care,
> And when he calls, the ready feast prepare.
> From wars and from affairs of state abstain;
> Women emasculate a monarch's reign,   200

---

173. *cozen*] cheat.

And murmuring crowds, who see 'em shine with gold,
That pomp as their own ravished spoils behold.
NOURMAHAL (*aside*).
    Rage chokes my words; 'tis womanly to weep.
    In my swoll'n breast my close revenge I'll keep;
    I'll watch his tender'st part, and there strike deep.   205
                                                    Exit.

AURENG-ZEBE.
    Your strange proceeding does my wonder move,
    Yet seems not to express a brother's love.
    Say to what cause my rescued life I owe.
MORAT.
    If what you ask would please, you should not know.
    But since that knowledge more than death will grieve,   210
    Know Indamora gained you this reprieve.
AURENG-ZEBE.
    And whence had she the pow'r to work your change?
MORAT.
    The pow'r of beauty is not new or strange.
    Should she command me more I could obey,
    But her request was bounded with a day.   215
    Take that, and if you'll spare my farther crime,
    Be kind and grieve to death against your time.

                Enter Arimant.

    Remove this pris'ner to some safer place.
    He has, for Indamora's sake, found grace,
    And from my mother's rage must guarded be   220
    Till you receive a new command from me.
ARIMANT (*aside*).
    Thus love and fortune persecute me still,
    And make me slave to every rival's will.
AURENG-ZEBE.
    How I disdain a life which I must buy
    With your contempt and her inconstancy!   225
    For a few hours, my whole content I pay.
    You shall not force on me another day.
                            Exit with Arimant.

---

216. *if you'll spare*] if you wish to prevent.
217. *against*] in advance of.

Enter Melesinda.

MELESINDA.

 I have been seeking you this hour's long space,
 And feared to find you in another place.
 But since you're here my jealousy grows less;   230
 You will be kind to my unworthiness.
 What shall I say? I love to that degree
 Each glance another way is robbed from me.
 Absence and prisons I could bear again,
 But sink and die beneath your least disdain.   235

MORAT.

 Why do you give your mind this needless care,
 And for yourself and me new pains prepare?
 I ne'er approved this passion in excess;
 If you would show your love, distrust me less.
 I hate to be pursued from place to place;   240
 Meet at each turn a stale domestic face.
 Th'approach of jealousy love cannot bear;
 He's wild, and soon on wing if watchful eyes come near.

MELESINDA.

 From your loved presence how can I depart?
 My eyes pursue the object of my heart.   245

MORAT.

 You talk as if it were our bridal night.
 Fondness is still th'effect of new delight,
 And marriage but the pleasure of a day;
 The metal's base, the gilding worn away.

MELESINDA.

 I fear I'm guilty of some great offense,   250
 And that has bred this cold indifference.

MORAT.

 The greatest in the world to flesh and blood:
 You fondly love much longer than you should.

MELESINDA.

 If that be all which makes your discontent,
 Of such a crime I never can repent.   255

MORAT.

 Would you force love upon me which I shun,

243. eyes] *Q 1–2, 4–6*; lies *Q 3*.

And bring coarse fare when appetite is gone?

MELESINDA.

Why did I not in prison die, before
My fatal freedom made me suffer more?
I had been pleased to think I died for you,   260
And doubly pleased because you then were true.
Then I had hope, but now, alas, have none.

MORAT.

You say you love me; let that love be shown.
'Tis in your power to make my happiness.

MELESINDA.

Speak quickly: to command me is to bless.   265

MORAT.

To Indamora you my suit must move;
You'll sure speak kindly of the man you love.

MELESINDA.

Oh, rather let me perish by your hand
Than break my heart by this unkind command!
Think 'tis the only one I could deny,   270
And that 'tis harder to refuse than die.
Try, if you please, my rival's heart to win;
I'll bear the pain, but not promote the sin.
You own whate'er perfections man can boast,
And if she view you with my eyes, she's lost.   275

MORAT.

Here I renounce all love, all nuptial ties;
Henceforth live a stranger to my eyes.
When I appear, see you avoid the place,
And haunt me not with that unlucky face.

MELESINDA.

Hard as it is, I this command obey,   280
And haste, while I have life, to go away.
In pity stay some hours, till I am dead,
That blameless you may court my rival's bed.
My hated face I'll not presume to show,
Yet I may watch your steps where'er you go.   285
Unseen I'll gaze, and with my latest breath
Bless, while I die, the author of my death.   *Weeping.*

Enter Emperor.

EMPEROR.

When your triumphant fortune high appears,
What cause can draw these unbecoming tears?
Let cheerfulness on happy fortune wait,   290
And give not thus the counter-time to fate.

MELESINDA.

Fortune long frowned, and has but lately smiled;
I doubt a foe so newly reconciled.
You saw but sorrow in its waning form,
A working sea remaining from a storm;   295
When the now weary waves roll o'er the deep,
And faintly murmur ere they fall asleep.

EMPEROR.

Your inward griefs you smother in your mind,
But fame's loud voice proclaims your lord unkind.

MORAT.

Let fame be busy where she has to do: 300
Tell of fought fields and every pompous show.
Those tales are fit to fill the people's ears;
Monarchs, unquestioned, move in higher spheres.

MELESINDA.

Believe not rumor, but yourself, and see
The kindness 'twixt my plighted lord and me.   305

Kissing Morat.

This is our state; thus happily we live;
These are the quarrels which we take and give.—
(*Aside to* Morat.)   I had no other way to force a kiss.
Forgive my last farewell to you, and bliss.   *Exit.*

EMPEROR.

Your haughty carriage shows too much of scorn,   310
And love like hers deserves not that return.

MORAT.

You'll please to leave me judge of what I do,
And not examine by the outward show.

299. fame's] *Q 1–2, 4–6*; fate's *Q 3.*

---

291. *counter-time*] a thrust made at an inopportune moment (*OED*, which cites this passage).
295. *working*] agitated.
301. *pompous*] magnificent.

Your usage of my mother might be good;
I judged it not.
EMPEROR.   Nor was it fit you should.   315
MORAT.
Then as in equal balance weigh my deeds.
EMPEROR.
My right and my authority exceeds.
Suppose (what I'll not grant) injustice done;
Is judging me the duty of a son?
MORAT.
Not of a son, but of an emperor;   320
You canceled duty when you gave me pow'r.
If your own actions on your will you ground,
Mine shall hereafter know no other bound.
What meant you when you called me to a throne?
Was it to please me with a name alone?   325
EMPEROR.
'Twas that I thought your gratitude would know
What to my partial kindness you did owe;
That what your birth did to your claim deny,
Your merit of obedience might supply.
MORAT.
To your own thoughts such hopes you might propose,   330
But I took empire not on terms like those.
Of business you complained; now take your ease;
Enjoy whate'er decrepid age can please:
Eat, sleep, and tell long tales of what you were
In flow'r of youth, if anyone will hear.   335
EMPEROR.
Pow'r, like new wine, does your weak brain surprise,
And its mad fumes in hot discourses rise.
But time these giddy vapors will remove;
Meanwhile I'll taste the sober joys of love.
MORAT.
You cannot love nor pleasures take, or give,   340
But life begin when 'tis too late to live.
On a tired courser you pursue delight,
Let slip your morning and set out at night.
If you have lived, take thankfully the past;
Make as you can the sweet remembrance last.   345

If you have not enjoyed what youth could give,
But life sunk through you like a leaky sieve,
Accuse yourself you lived not while you might;
But in the captive queen resign your right.
I've now resolved to fill your useless place;   350
I'll take that post to cover your disgrace,
And love her for the honor of my race.

EMPEROR.

Thou dost but try how far I can forbear,
Nor art that monster which thou wouldst appear.
But do not wantonly my passion move;   355
I pardon nothing that relates to love.
My fury does, like jealous forts, pursue
With death ev'n strangers who but come to view.

MORAT.

I did not only view, but will invade.
Could you shed venom from your reverend shade   360
Like trees beneath whose arms 'tis death to sleep,
Did rolling thunder your fenced fortress keep,
Thence would I snatch my Semele, like Jove,
And midst the dreadful wrack enjoy my love.

EMPEROR.

Have I for this, ungrateful as thou art,   365
When right, when nature struggled in my heart,
When Heav'n called on me for thy brother's claim,
Broke all, and sullied my unspotted fame?
Wert thou to empire by my baseness brought,
And wouldst thou ravish what so dear I bought?   370
Dear! For my conscience and its peace I gave.
Why was my reason made my passion's slave?
I see Heav'n's justice: thus the pow'rs divine
Pay crimes with crimes, and punish mine by thine.

364. rack] *Q 1–2, 4*; wrack *Q 3,
5–6.*

357. *jealous*] watchful.
361.] The yew was supposed by Dioscorides and Pliny to poison those
who lingered beneath it.
363. *Semele*] Juno tricked Semele into obtaining Jupiter's promise to
appear before her undisguised; the splendor consumed her.

MORAT.

    Crimes let them pay, and punish as they please;   375
    What pow'r makes mine, by pow'r I mean to seize.
    Since 'tis to that they their own greatness owe
    Above, why should they question mine below?   *Exit.*

EMPEROR.

    Prudence, thou vainly in our youth art sought,
    And with age purchased art too dearly bought.   380
    We're past the use of wit, for which we toil;
    Late fruit, and planted in too cold a soil.
    My stock of fame is lavished and decayed,
    No profit of the vast profusion made.
    Too late my folly I repent; I know   385
    My Aureng-Zebe would ne'er have used me so.
    But by his ruin I prepared my own,
    And like a naked tree, my shelter gone,
    To winds and winter storms must stand exposed alone.   *Exit.*

[IV.ii]   [*Enter*] Aureng-Zebe, Arimant.

ARIMANT.

    Give me not thanks, which I will ne'er deserve,
    But know, 'tis for a nobler price I serve.
    By Indamora's will you're hither brought;
    All my reward in her command I sought.
    The rest your letter tells you. See, like light   5
    She comes, and I must vanish like the night.   *Exit.*

Enter Indamora.

INDAMORA.

    'Tis now that I begin to live again;
    Heav'ns, I forgive you all my fear and pain.
    Since I behold my Aureng-Zebe appear,
    I could not buy him at a price too dear.   10
    His name alone afforded me relief,
    Repeated as a charm to cure my grief.

379. art] *Q 1–2, 4–6*; are *Q 3*.   [IV.ii]
                          5. letter tells] *Q 1*; letters tell
                          Q 2–6.

  I that loved name did, as some god, invoke,
  And printed kisses on it while I spoke.

AURENG-ZEBE.

  Short ease, but long, long pains from you I find: 15
  Health to my eyes, but poison to my mind.
  Why are you made so excellently fair?
  So much above what other beauties are
  That ev'n in cursing, you new form my breath,
  And make me bless those eyes which give me death? 20

INDAMORA.

  What reason for your curses can you find?
  My eyes your conquest, not your death, designed.
  If they offend, 'tis that they are too kind.

AURENG-ZEBE.

  The ruins they have wrought you will not see.
  Too kind they are indeed, but not to me.   25

INDAMORA.

  Think you base interest souls like mine can sway?
  Or that for greatness I can love betray?
  No, Aureng-Zebe, you merit all my heart,
  And I'm too noble but to give a part.
  Your father, and an empire! Am I known   30
  No more? Or have so weak a judgment shown
  In choosing you, to change you for a throne?

AURENG-ZEBE.

  How, with a truth, you would a falsehood blind!
  'Tis not my father's love you have designed;
  Your choice is fixed where youth and pow'r are joined. 35

INDAMORA.

  Where youth and pow'r are joined! Has he a name?

AURENG-ZEBE.

  You would be told; you glory in your shame.
  There's music in the sound, and to provoke
  Your pleasure more, by me it must be spoke.
  Then, then it ravishes, when your pleased ear 40
  The sound does from a wretched rival hear.

22. your death] *Q 1–2, 4–6*; you
death *Q 3*.

Morat's the name your heart leaps up to meet,
While Aureng-Zebe lies dying at your feet.

INDAMORA.

Who told you this?

AURENG-ZEBE.   Are you so lost to shame?
Morat, Morat, Morat! You love the name   45
So well your ev'ry question ends in that;
You force me still to answer you, Morat.
Morat, who best could tell what you revealed;
Morat, too proud to keep his joy concealed.

INDAMORA.

Howe'er unjust your jealousy appear,   50
It shows the loss of what you love, you fear,
And does my pity, not my anger, move;
I'll fond it as the froward child of love.
To show the truth of my unaltered breast,
Know that your life was given at my request—   55
At least reprieved. When Heav'n denied you aid,
She brought it; she whose falsehood you upbraid.

AURENG-ZEBE.

And 'tis by that you would your falsehood hide.
Had you not asked, how happy had I died!
Accurst reprieve, not to prolong my breath;   60
It brought a ling'ring and more painful death.
I have not lived since first I heard the news;
The gift the guilty giver does accuse.
You knew the price, and the request did move
That you might pay the ransom with your love.   65

INDAMORA.

Your accusation must, I see, take place,
And I am guilty, infamous, and base!

AURENG-ZEBE.

If you are false those epithets are small;
You're then the things, the abstract of 'em all.
And you are false: you promised him your love.   70
No other price so hard a heart could move.

49. joy] *Q 1-2, 4-6*; joys *Q 3*.   66. accusation] *Q 1-2, 4-6*; accusations *Q 3*.

53. *fond . . . froward*] fondle . . . willful.

Do I not know him? Could his brutal mind
Be wrought upon? Could he be just, or kind?
Insultingly he made your love his boast;
Gave me my life, and told me what it cost.　　　　75
Speak! Answer! I would fain yet think you true.
Lie, and I'll not believe myself, but you.
Tell me you love; I'll pardon the deceit,
And, to be fooled, myself assist the cheat.

INDAMORA.

No, 'tis too late; I have no more to say.　　　　80
If you'll believe I have been false, you may.

AURENG-ZEBE.

I would not, but your crimes too plain appear;
Nay, even that I should think you true, you fear.
Did I not tell you I would be deceived?

INDAMORA.

I'm not concerned to have my truth believed.　　　　85
You would be cozened! Would assist the cheat!
But I'm too plain to join in the deceit.
I'm pleased you think me false,
And whatsoe'er my letter did pretend,
I made this meeting for no other end.　　　　90

AURENG-ZEBE.

Kill me not quite with this indifference;
When you are guiltless, boast not an offense.
I know you better than yourself you know:
Your heart was true, but did some frailty show.
You promised him your love that I might live,　　　　95
But promised what you never meant to give.
Speak, was't not so? Confess; I can forgive.

INDAMORA.

Forgive! What dull excuses you prepare!
As if your thoughts of me were worth my care.

AURENG-ZEBE.

Ah, traitress! Ah, ingrate! Ah, faithless mind!　　　　100
Ah, sex invented first to damn mankind!
Nature took care to dress you up for sin:
Adorned without, unfinished left within.
Hence by no judgment you your loves direct;

Talk much, ne'er think, and still the wrong affect.   105
So much self-love in your composures mixed
That love to others still remains unfixed.
Greatness and noise and show are your delight,
Yet wise men love you in their own despite;
And finding in their native wit no ease,   110
Are forced to put your folly on to please.

INDAMORA.

Now you shall know what cause you have to rage,
But to increase your fury, not assuage:
I found the way your brother's heart to move,
Yet promised not the least return of love.   115
His pride and brutal fierceness I abhor,
But scorn your mean suspicions of me more.
I owed my honor and my fame this care;
Know what your folly lost you, and despair.

Turning from him.

AURENG-ZEBE.

Too cruelly your innocence you tell,   120
Show Heav'n, and damn me to the pit of hell.
Now I believe you, 'tis not yet too late;
You may forgive, and put a stop to fate:
Save me, just sinking, and no more to rise.   *She frowns.*
How can you look with such relentless eyes?   125
Or let your mind by penitence be moved,
Or I'm resolved to think you never loved.
You are not cleared unless you mercy speak;
I'll think you took th'occasion thus to break.

INDAMORA.

Small jealousies, 'tis true, inflame desire;   130
Too great, not fan, but quite blow out the fire.
Yet I did love you, till such pains I bore
That I dare trust myself and you no more.
Let me not love you, but here end my pain;
Distrust may make me wretched once again.   135
Now with full sails into the port I move,
And safely can unlade my breast of love,

105. affect] *Q 1*; effect *Q 2–6*.   117. scorn] *Q 1, 3–6*; corn *Q 2*.
107. remains] *Q 1–2*; remain *Q 3–6*.   124. me] *Q 1–4*; *om. Q 5–6*.
109. you] *Q 1, 3*; *om. Q 2, 4–6*.

Quiet and calm. Why should I then go back
To tempt the second hazard of a wrack?

AURENG-ZEBE.

Behold these dying eyes, see their submissive awe;   140
These tears, which fear of death could never draw.
Heard you that sigh? From my heaved heart it passed,
And said, if you forgive not, 'tis my last.
Love mounts and rolls about my stormy mind
Like fire that's borne by a tempestuous wind.   145
Oh, I could stifle you with eager haste!
Devour your kisses with my hungry taste!
Rush on you! Eat you! Wander o'er each part,
Raving with pleasure, snatch you to my heart!
Then hold you off and gaze! Then, with new rage   150
Invade you, till my conscious limbs presage
Torrents of joy which all their banks o'erflow!
So lost, so blest as I but then could know!

INDAMORA (*giving him her hand*).
Be no more jealous.

AURENG-ZEBE.   Give me cause no more.
The danger's greater after than before.   155
If I relapse, to cure my jealousy
Let me (for that's the easiest parting) die.

INDAMORA.
My life!

AURENG-ZEBE. My soul!

INDAMORA.   My all that Heav'n can give!
Death's life with you; without you, death to live.

To them Arimant *hastily.*

ARIMANT.
Oh, we are lost, beyond all human aid!   160
The Citadel is to Morat betrayed.
The traitor and the treason known too late;
The false Abas delivered up the gate.
Ev'n while I speak we're compassed round with fate.

138. Quiet] *Q 1–2, 4–6*; Quite *Q 3.*   162. known] *Q 1–2, 4*; know *Q 3,
5–6.*

The valiant cannot fight or coward fly,   165
But both in undistinguished crowds must die.

AURENG-ZEBE.

Then my prophetic fears are come to pass:
Morat was always bloody; now he's base,
And has so far in usurpation gone
He will by parricide secure the throne.   170

To them the Emperor.

EMPEROR.

Am I forsaken and betrayed by all?
Not one brave man dare with a monarch fall?
Then welcome death, to cover my disgrace;
I would not live to reign o'er such a race.—
(*Seeing* Aureng-Zebe.)   My Aureng-Zebe!   175
But thou no more art mine; my cruelty
Has quite destroyed the right I had in thee.
I have been base,
Base ev'n to him from whom I did receive
All that a son could to a parent give.   180
Behold me punished in the selfsame kind:
Th'ungrateful does a more ungrateful find.

AURENG-ZEBE.

Accuse youself no more. You could not be
Ungrateful, could commit no crime to me.
I only mourn my yet uncanceled score;   185
You put me past the pow'r of paying more.
That, that's my grief, that I can only grieve,
And bring but pity where I would relieve.
For had I yet ten thousand lives to pay,
The mighty sum should go no other way.   190

EMPEROR.

Can you forgive me? 'Tis not fit you should.
Why will you be so excellently good?
'Twill stick too black a brand upon my name.
The sword is needless; I shall die with shame.
What had my age to do with love's delight,   195
Shut out from all enjoyments but the sight?

ARIMANT.

    Sir, you forget the danger's imminent;
    This minute is not for excuses lent.

EMPEROR.

    Disturb me not.
    How can my latest hour be better spent?   200
    To reconcile myself to him is more
    Than to regain all I possessed before.
    Empire and life are now not worth a pray'r;
    His love alone deserves my dying care.

AURENG-ZEBE.

    Fighting for you, my death will glorious be.   205

INDAMORA.

    Seek to preserve yourself, and live for me.

ARIMANT.

    Lose then no farther time.
    Heav'n has inspired me with a sudden thought
    Whence your unhoped-for safety may be wrought,
    Though with the hazard of my blood 'tis bought.   210
    But since my life can ne'er be fortunate,
    'Tis so much sorrow well redeemed from fate.—
    [*To* Indamora.]   You, madam, must retire
    (Your beauty is its own security),
    And leave the conduct of the rest to me.   215
    Glory will crown my life if I succeed—
    (*Aside.*)   If not, she may afford to love me dead.

AURENG-ZEBE.

    My father's kind, and, madam, you forgive;
    Were Heav'n so pleased, I now could wish to live.
    And I shall live.   220
    With glory and with love at once I burn;
    I feel th'inspiring heat and absent god return.

                                        Exeunt.

200. hour] *Q 1–2*; hours *Q 3–6*.

  200. *latest*] last.

ACT V

Indamora *alone.*

[INDAMORA.]

The night seems doubled with the fear she brings,
And o'er the Citadel new-spreads her wings.
The morning, as mistaken, turns about,
And all her early fires again go out.
Shouts, cries, and groans first pierce my ears, and then   5
A flash of lightning draws the guilty scene,
And shows me arms and wounds and dying men.
Ah, should my Aureng-Zebe be fighting there,
And envious winds distinguished to my ear
His dying groans, and his last accents bear!   10

To her Morat, *attended.*

MORAT.

The bloody bus'ness of the night is done,
And, in the Citadel, an empire won.
Our swords so wholly did the fates employ
That they at length grew weary to destroy;
Refused the work we brought, and, out of breath,   15
Made sorrow and despair attend for death.
But what of all my conquest can I boast?
My haughty pride before your eyes is lost,
And victory but gains me to present
That homage which our eastern world has sent.   20

INDAMORA.

Your victory, alas, begets my fears.
Can you not then triumph without my tears?
Resolve me (for you know my destiny
Is Aureng-Zebe's); say, do I live or die?

MORAT.

Urged by my love, by hope of empire fired,   25
'Tis true, I have performed what both required,
What fate decreed; for when great souls are giv'n,
They bear the marks of sov'reignty from Heav'n.

---

3. *as*] as if.
23. *Resolve*] tell.

My elder brothers my forerunners came,
Rough draughts of nature, ill designed, and lame;   30
Blown off like blossoms, never made to bear;
Till I came, finished, her last labored care.

INDAMORA.

This prologue leads to your succeeding sin;
Blood ended what ambition did begin.

MORAT.

'Twas rumored, but by whom I cannot tell,   35
My father 'scaped from out the Citadel.
My brother too may live.

INDAMORA.   He may?
MORAT.   He must.
I killed him not, and a less fate's unjust.
Heav'n owes it me, that I may fill his room;
A phoenix lover rising from his tomb,   40
In whom you'll lose your sorrows for the dead;
More warm, more fierce, and fitter for your bed.

INDAMORA.

Should I from Aureng-Zebe my heart divide
To love a monster and a parricide?
These names your swelling titles cannot hide.   45
Severe decrees may keep our tongues in awe,
But to our thoughts what edict can give law?
Ev'n you yourself to your own breast shall tell
Your crimes, and your own conscience be your hell.

MORAT.

What bus'ness has my conscience with a crown?   50
She sinks in pleasures, and in bowls will drown.
If mirth should fail I'll busy her with cares,
Silence her clamorous voice with louder wars:
Trumpets and drums shall fright her from the throne,
As sounding cymbals aid the lab'ring moon.   55

INDAMORA.

Repelled by these, more eager she will grow;

---

40. *phoenix . . . tomb*] The phoenix was said to regenerate itself periodically from the ashes of its own funeral pyre.
51. *bowls*] of wine.
55. *As . . . moon*] Loud noises were primitively supposed to bring the moon out of an eclipse.

Spring back more strongly than a Scythian bow.
Amidst your train this unseen judge will wait,
Examine how you came by all your state,
Upbraid your impious pomp, and in your ear   60
Will hallow, "Rebel! Tyrant! Murderer!"
Your ill-got pow'r wan looks and care shall bring:
Known but by discontent to be a king.
Of crowds afraid, yet anxious when alone,
You'll sit and brood your sorrows on a throne.   65

MORAT.

Birthright's a vulgar road to kingly sway;
'Tis ev'ry dull-got elder brother's way.
Dropped from above, he lights into a throne,
Grows of a piece with that he sits upon;
Heav'n's choice, a low, inglorious, rightful drone.   70
But who by force a scepter does obtain,
Shows he can govern that which he could gain.
Right comes of course, whate'er he was before;
Murder and usurpation are no more.

INDAMORA.

By your own laws you such dominion make   75
As ev'ry stronger pow'r has right to take,
And parricide will so deform your name
That dispossessing you will give a claim.
Who next usurps will a just prince appear,
So much your ruin will his reign endear.   80

MORAT.

I without guilt would mount the royal seat,
But yet 'tis necessary to be great.

INDAMORA.

All greatness is in virtue understood;
'Tis only necessary to be good.

61. hallow] *Q 1-3*; hollow *Q 4-6*.

---

57. *Scythian*] The Scythians were fierce nomadic tribes of European and
Asiatic Russia.
  61. *hallow*] shout.
  70. *rightful*] legal.
  73. *of course*] as a matter of course.

Tell me, what is't at which great spirits aim,   85
What most yourself desire?

MORAT.   Renown, and fame,
And pow'r as uncontrolled as is my will.

INDAMORA.

How you confound desires of good and ill!
For true renown is still with virtue joined,
But lust of pow'r lets loose th'unbridled mind.   90
Yours is a soul irregularly great,
Which, wanting temper, yet abounds with heat,
So strong yet so unequal pulses beat;
A sun which does through vapors dimly shine.
What pity 'tis you are not all divine!   95
New molded, thorough lightened, and a breast
So pure to bear the last severest test;
Fit to command an empire you should gain
By virtue, and without a blush to reign.

MORAT.

You show me somewhat I ne'er learnt before,   100
But 'tis the distant prospect of a shore
Doubtful in mists, which, like enchanted ground,
Flies from my sight before 'tis fully found.

INDAMORA.

Dare to be great without a guilty crown;
View it, and lay the bright temptation down.   105
'Tis base to seize on all because you may;
That's empire, that which I can give away.
There's joy when to wild will you laws prescribe,
When you bid fortune carry back her bribe;
A joy which none but greatest minds can taste,   110
A fame which will to endless ages last.

MORAT.

Renown and fame in vain I courted long,
And still pursued 'em, though directed wrong.
In hazard and in toils I heard they lay,
Sailed farther than the coast, but missed my way.   115
Now you have giv'n me virtue for my guide,

109. bribe] *Q 1*; bride *Q 2–6*.   110. which] *Q 1–2, 4–6*; when *Q 3*.

96. *thorough lightened*] fully enlightened.

And with true honor ballasted my pride.
Unjust dominion I no more pursue;
I quit all other claims but those to you.

INDAMORA.

Oh, be not just to halves! Pay all you owe;   120
Think there's a debt to Melesinda too.
To leave no blemish on your after life,
Reward the virtue of a suff'ring wife.

MORAT.

To love once past I cannot backward move;
Call yesterday again, and I may love.   125
'Twas not for nothing I the crown resigned;
I still must own a mercenary mind:
I in this venture double gains pursue,
And laid out all my stock to purchase you.

To them Asaph Chan.

Now, what success? Does Aureng-Zebe yet live?   130

ASAPH.

Fortune has giv'n you all that she can give.
Your brother—

MORAT.   Hold! Thou show'st an impious joy,
And think'st I still take pleasure to destroy.
Know I am changed, and would not have him slain.

ASAPH.

'Tis past, and you desire his life in vain.   135
He, prodigal of soul, rushed on the stroke
Of lifted weapons, and did wounds provoke.
In scorn of night, he would not be concealed;
His soldiers, where he fought, his name revealed.
In thickest crowds still "Aureng-Zebe" did sound,   140
The vaulted roofs did "Aureng-Zebe" rebound.
Till late, and in his fall, the name was drowned.

INDAMORA.

Wither that hand which brought him to his fate,
And blasted be the tongue which did relate.

ASAPH.

His body—

MORAT.   Cease to enhance her misery.   145

143. Wither] *Q 1–3*; whither *Q 4–6*.

―99―

Pity the Queen, and show respect to me.
'Tis ev'ry painter's art to hide from sight
And cast in shades what, seen, would not delight.—
(*To her.*)   Your grief in me such sympathy has bred,
I mourn, and wish I could recall the dead.   150
Love softens me, and blows up fires which pass
Through my tough heart and melt the stubborn mass.

INDAMORA.

Break, heart, or choke with sobs my hated breath;
Do thy own work; admit no foreign death.
Alas! Why do I make this useless moan?   155
I'm dead already, for my soul is gone.

To them Mir Baba.

MIR BABA.

What tongue the terror of this night can tell,
Within, without, and round the Citadel!
A new-formed faction does your pow'r oppose;
The fight's confused, and all who meet are foes.   160
A second clamor from the town we hear,
And the far noise so loud it drowns the near.
Abas, who seemed our friend, is either fled
Or, what we fear, our enemies does head.
Your frighted soldiers scarce their ground maintain.   165

MORAT.

I thank their fury; we shall fight again.
They rouse my rage; I'm eager to subdue—
'Tis fatal to withhold my eyes from you.

Exit with the two Omrahs.

Enter Melesinda.

MELESINDA.

Can misery no place of safety know?
The noise pursues me wheresoe'er I go,   170
As fate sought only me, and where I fled,
Aimed all its darts at my devoted head.
And let it. I am now past care of life;
The last of women, an abandoned wife.

INDAMORA.

   Whether design or chance has brought you here,   175
   I stand obliged to fortune or to fear:
   Weak women should, in danger, herd like deer.
   But say from whence this new combustion springs?
   Are there yet more Morats? More fighting kings?

MELESINDA.

   Him from his mother's love your eyes divide,   180
   And now her arms the cruel strife decide.

INDAMORA.

   What strange misfortunes my vexed life attend!
   Death will be kind, and all my sorrows end.
   If Nourmahal prevail, I know my fate.

MELESINDA.

   I pity as my own your hard estate,   185
   But what can my weak charity afford?
   I have no longer int'rest in my lord,
   Nor in his mother, he; she owns her hate
   Aloud, and would herself usurp the state.

INDAMORA.

   I'm stupified with sorrow, past relief   190
   Of tears; parched up, and withered with my grief.

MELESINDA.

   Dry mourning will decays more deadly bring,
   As a north wind burns a too forward spring.
   Give sorrow vent, and let the sluices go.

INDAMORA.

   My tears are all congealed, and will not flow.   195

MELESINDA.

   Have comfort; yield not to the blows of fate.

INDAMORA.

   Comfort, like cordials after death, comes late.
   Name not so vain a word; my hopes are fled.
   Think your Morat were kind, and think him dead.

MELESINDA.

   I can no more—   200
   Can no more arguments for comfort find,

---

177. herd] *Q 1–2, 4–6*; heard *Q 3*.   194. go] *Q 1–2, 4–6*; no *Q 3*.

197. *cordials*] restoratives.

Your boding words have quite o'erwhelmed my mind.

Clattering of weapons within.

INDAMORA.

The noise increases, as the billows roar
When rolling from afar they threat the shore.
She comes; and feeble nature now I find   205
Shrinks back in danger and forsakes my mind.
I wish to die, yet dare not death endure;
Detest the med'cine, yet desire the cure.
I would have death, but mild, and at command;
I dare not trust him in another's hand.   210
In Nourmahal's, he would not mine appear,
But armed with terror and disguised with fear.

MELESINDA.

Beyond this place you can have no retreat.
Stay here, and I the danger will repeat.
I fear not death, because my life I hate,   215
And envious death will shun th'unfortunate.

INDAMORA.

You must not venture.

MELESINDA.   Let me; I may do
Myself a kindness in obliging you.
In your loved name I'll seek my angry lord,
And beg your safety from his conqu'ring sword.   220
So his protection all your fears will ease,
And I shall see him once, and not displease.   *Exit.*

INDAMORA.

Oh wretched Queen! What pow'r thy life can save?
A stranger, and unfriended, and a slave!

Enter Nourmahal, Zayda, *and* Abas, *with soldiers.*

Alas, she's here!   225
Indamora withdraws to the inner part of the scene.

NOURMAHAL.

Heartless they fought, and quitted soon their ground,
While ours with easy victory were crowned.
To you, Abas, my life and empire too,
And, what's yet dearer, my revenge, I owe.

ABAS.

The vain Morat, by his own rashness wrought,   230

Too soon discovered his ambitious thought;
Believed me his because I spoke him fair,
And pitched his head into the ready snare.
Hence 'twas I did his troops at first admit,
But such, whose numbers could no fears beget;   235
By them th'Emperor's party first I slew,
Then turned my arms the victors to subdue.

NOURMAHAL.

Now let the headstrong boy my will control!
Virtue's no slave of man; no sex confines the soul.
I for myself th'imperial seat will gain,   240
And he shall wait my leisure for his reign.
But Aureng-Zebe is nowhere to be found.
And now perhaps in death's cold arms he lies;
I fought and conquered, yet have lost the prize.

ZAYDA.

The chance of war determined well the strife   245
That racked you, 'twixt the lover and the wife.
He's dead, whose love had sullied all your reign,
And made you Empress of the world in vain.

NOURMAHAL.

No, I my pow'r and pleasure would divide:
The drudge had quenched my flames, and then had died. 250
I rage to think without that bliss I live;
That I could wish what fortune would not give.
But what love cannot, vengeance must supply;
She who bereaved me of his heart shall die.

ZAYDA.

I'll search. Far distant hence she cannot be.   *Goes in.* 255

NOURMAHAL.

This wondrous masterpiece I fain would see;
This fatal Helen, who can wars inspire,
Make kings her slaves, and set the world on fire.
My husband locked his jewel from my view,
Or durst not set the false one by the true.   260

255.S.D. *Goes*] *Q 1–2, 4–5; Going*
Q 3, 6.

239. *no . . . soul*] courage is not limited by sex.

Re-enter Zayda, *leading* Indamora.

ZAYDA.
Your frighted captive, ere she dies, receive;
Her soul's just going else, without your leave.

NOURMAHAL.
A fairer creature did my eyes ne'er see!
Sure she was formed by Heav'n in spite to me!
Some angel copied, while I slept, each grace,   265
And molded ev'ry feature from my face.
Such majesty does from her forehead rise,
Her cheeks such blushes cast, such rays her eyes,
Nor I, nor envy, can a blemish find.
The palace is, without, too well designed;   270
Conduct me in, for I will view thy mind.—
(*To her.*)   Speak, if thou hast a soul, that I may see
If Heav'n can make throughout another me.

INDAMORA (*kneeling*).
My tears and miseries must plead my cause;
My words, the terror of your presence awes.   275
Mortals, in sight of angels, mute become:
The nobler nature strikes th'inferior dumb.

NOURMAHAL.
The palm is, by the foe's confession, mine,
But I disdain what basely you resign.
Heav'n did, by me, the outward model build;   280
Its inward work, the soul, with rubbish filled.
Yet oh, th'imperfect piece moves more delight;
'Tis gilded o'er with youth, to catch the sight.
The gods have poorly robbed my virgin bloom,
And what I am, by what I was, o'ercome.   285
Traitress, restore my beauty and my charms,
Nor steal my conquests with my proper arms.

INDAMORA.
What have I done, thus to inflame your hate?
I am not guilty, but unfortunate.

272. that] *Q 1–2, 4–6*; and that   273.] *om. Q 3, 5–6.*
Q 3.

287. *proper*] own.

NOURMAHAL.

Not guilty, when thy looks my pow'r betray,   290
Seduce mankind, my subject, from my sway,
Take all my hearts and all my eyes away?
My husband first, but that I could forgive;
He only moved and talked, but did not live.
My Aureng-Zebe—for I dare own the name,   295
The glorious sin, and the more glorious flame—
Him from my beauty have thy eyes misled,
And starved the joys of my expected bed.

INDAMORA.

His love so sought, he's happy that he's dead.
Oh had I courage but to meet my fate,   300
That short dark passage to a future state,
That melancholy riddle of a breath.

NOURMAHAL.

That something, or that nothing, after death.
Take this, and teach thyself.   *Giving a dagger.*

INDAMORA.

Alas!

NOURMAHAL. Why dost thou shake?   305
Dishonor not the vengeance I designed:
A queen, and own a base plebeian mind!
Let it drink deep in thy most vital part;
Strike home, and do me reason in thy heart.

INDAMORA.

I dare not.

NOURMAHAL.   Do't, while I stand by and see   310
At my full gust, without the drudgery.
I love a foe who dares my stroke prevent,
Who gives me the full scene of my content,
Shows me the flying soul's convulsive strife,
And all the anguish of departing life.   315
Disdain my mercy, and my rage defy;

291. subject] *Q 1–2, 4–6*; subjects   302. That] *Q 1–2, 4–6*; The *Q 3.*
Q 3.

---

309. *do me reason*] a pun: the phrase means both "drink to me" and "do
me justice."
311. *gust*] gusto, pleasure.
314. *flying*] departing.

Curse me with thy last breath, and make me see
A spirit worthy to have rivaled me.

INDAMORA.

Oh, I desire to die, but dare not yet;
Give me some respite, I'll discharge the debt.   320
Without my Aureng-Zebe I would not live.

NOURMAHAL.

Thine, traitress? Thine? That word has winged thy fate,
And put me past the tedious forms of hate.
I'll kill thee with such eagerness and haste
As fiends, let loose, would lay all nature waste.   325

Indamora *runs back as* Nourmahal *is running to her. Clashing of swords is heard within.*

SOLDIER (*within*).

Yield, y'are o'erpow'red! Resistance is in vain.

MORAT (*within*).

Then death's my choice; submission I disdain.

NOURMAHAL (*at the door*).

Retire, you slaves! Ah, whether does he run
On pointed swords? Disarm, but save my son!
                    Enter Morat *staggering, and upheld by soldiers.*

MORAT.

She lives! And I shall see her once again!   330
I have not thrown away my life in vain.
          Catches hold of Indamora's gown, and falls by her; she sits.
I can no more, yet ev'n in death I find
My fainting body biased by my mind:
I fall toward you; still my contending soul
Points to your breast, and trembles to its pole.   335

To them Melesinda, *hastily, casting herself on the other side of* Morat.

MELESINDA.

Ah, woe, woe, woe! The worst of woes I find!

321. would not] *Q 1–2, 4–6*; can-   328. whether] *Q 1*; whither *Q 2,*
not *Q 3*.   *4–6*; wither *Q 3*.

---

328. *whether*] whither.
333–335.] The first metaphor refers to the bias given a bowling ball;
the second refers to the compass needle.

Live still! Oh, live; live ev'n to be unkind!
With half-shut eyes he seeks the doubtful day,
But, ah, he bends his sight another way.
He faints! And in that sigh his soul is gone;   340
Yet Heaven's unmoved, yet Heav'n looks careless on!

NOURMAHAL.

Where are those pow'rs which monarchs should defend?
Or do they vain authority pretend
O'er human fates, and their weak empire show,
Which cannot guard their images below?   345
If, as their image, he was not divine,
They ought to have respected him as mine.
I'll waken them with my revenge; and she,
Their Indamora, shall my victim be,
And helpless Heav'n shall mourn in vain, like me.   350

As she is going to stab Indamora, Morat *raises himself, and holds her hand.*

MORAT.

Ah, what are we
Who dare maintain with Heav'n this wretched strife,
Puffed with the pride of Heav'n's own gift, frail life?
That blast which my ambitious spirit swelled,
See by how weak a tenure it was held!   355
I only stay to save the innocent;
Oh envy not my soul its last content.

INDAMORA.

No, let me die; I'm doubly summoned now:
First by my Aureng-Zebe, and since, by you.
My soul grows hardy, and can death endure;   360
Your convoy makes the dang'rous way secure.

MELESINDA.

Let me at least a funeral marriage crave,
Nor grudge my cold embraces in the grave.
I have too just a title in the strife:
By me, unhappy me, he lost his life.   365
I called him hither, 'twas my fatal breath;

337. live; live] *Q 1–2, 4*; live;   340. sigh] *Q 1–2, 4–5*; sight *Q 3,*
Q 3, 5–6.   *6.*

338. *doubtful day*] light (life) he may no longer have.

And I the screech owl that proclaimed his death.

Shout within.

ABAS.

What new alarms are these? I'll haste and see.   *Exit.*

NOURMAHAL.

Look up and live; an empire shall be thine.

MORAT.

That I contemned ev'n when I thought it mine.—   370
(*To* Indamora.)   Oh, I must yield to my hard destinies,
And must forever cease to see your eyes.

MELESINDA.

Ah, turn your sight to me, my dearest lord!
Can you not one, one parting look afford?
Ev'n so unkind in death? But 'tis in vain;   375
I lose my breath, and to the winds complain.
Yet 'tis as much in vain, your cruel scorn;
Still I can love, without this last return.
Nor fate nor you can my vowed faith control;
Dying, I'll follow your disdainful soul.   380
A ghost, I'll haunt your ghost, and where you go,
With mournful murmurs fill the plains below.

MORAT.

Be happy, Melesinda, cease to grieve,
And for a more deserving husband live.
Can you forgive me?

MELESINDA.   Can I! Oh, my heart!   385
Have I heard one kind word before I part?
I can, I can forgive; is that a task
To love like mine? Are you so good to ask?
One kiss—   (*Kisses him.*)   Oh, 'tis too great a blessing, this;
I would not live to violate the bliss.   390

Re-enter Abas.

ABAS.

Some envious devil has ruined us yet more:
The fort's revolted to the Emperor.
The gates are opened, the portcullis drawn,

367.1. *Shout*] *Q 1–2, 4; Shouts Q 3,*
5–6.

367. *screech owl*] commonly an omen of death.

And deluges of armies from the town
Come pow'ring in. I heard the mighty flaw   395
When first it broke; the crowding ensigns saw
Which choked the passage; and (what least I feared)
The waving arms of Aureng-Zebe appeared
Displayed with your Morat's.
In either's flag the golden serpents bear,   400
Erected crests alike, like volumes rear,
And mingle friendly hissings in the air.
Their troops are joined, and our destruction nigh.

NOURMAHAL.

'Tis vain to fight, and I disdain to fly.
I'll mock the triumphs which our foes intend,   405
And spite of fortune make a glorious end.
In pois'nous draughts my liberty I'll find,
And from the nauseous world set free my mind.   *Exit.*

At the other end of the stage enter Aureng-Zebe, Dianet, *and attendants.*
Aureng-Zebe *turns back and speaks, ent'ring.*

AURENG-ZEBE.

The lives of all who cease from combat spare;
My brother's be your most peculiar care.   410
Our impious use no longer shall obtain:
Brothers no more by brothers shall be slain.
                                   Seeing Indamora *and* Morat.
Ha! Do I dream? Is this my hoped success?
I grow a statue, stiff and motionless.
Look, Dianet, for I dare not trust these eyes;   415
They dance in mists, and dazzle with surprise.

DIANET.

Sir, 'tis Morat. Dying he seems, or dead,
And Indamora's hand—

AURENG-ZEBE (*sighing*).   Supports his head.
Thou shalt not break yet, heart, nor shall she know
My inward torments by my outward show.   420
To let her see my weakness were too base;

---

395. *flaw*] uproar.
398. *arms*] insignia.
400. *bear*] appear.

−109−

Dissembled quiet sit upon my face:
My sorrow to my eyes no passage find,
But let it inward sink, and drown my mind.
Falsehood shall want its triumph. I begin   425
To stagger, but I'll prop myself within.
The specious tow'r no ruin shall disclose,
Till down at once the mighty fabric goes.

MORAT (*to* Indamora).
In sign that I die yours, reward my love,
And seal my passport to the blessed above.   430
                                        Kissing her hand.

INDAMORA.
Oh stay, or take me with you when you go;
There's nothing now worth living for below.

MORAT.
I leave you not, for my expanded mind
Grows up to Heav'n while it to you is joined;
Not quitting, but enlarged! A blazing fire   435
Fed from the brand.   *Dies.*

MELESINDA.
Ah me! He's gone! I die!   *Swoons.*

INDAMORA.   Oh dismal day!
Fate, thou hast ravished my last hope away.
            She turns and sees Aureng-Zebe *standing by her, and starts.*
Oh Heav'n! My Aureng-Zebe! What strange surprise!
Or does my willing mind delude my eyes,   440
And shows the figure always present there?
Or liv'st thou? Am I blessed, and see thee here?

AURENG-ZEBE (*turning from her to his attendants*).
My brother's body see conveyed with care
Where we may royal sepulture prepare.
With speed to Melesinda bring relief;   445
Recall her spirits, and moderate her grief.
                                    Half turning to Indamora.

427. specious] *Q 1–2, 4–5;* spacious
Q 3, 6.

427. *specious*] deceptively sound.

I go, to take forever from your view
Both the loved object and the hated too.
                    Going away after the bodies, which are carried off.
INDAMORA *(laying hold of him).*

Hear me, yet think not that I beg your stay;
I will be heard, and after take your way.   450
Go; but your late repentance shall be vain:
                    He struggles still; she lets him go.
I'll never, never see your face again.   *Turning away.*
AURENG-ZEBE.

Madam, I know whatever you can say;
You might be pleased not to command my stay.
All things are yet disordered in the fort;   455
I must crave leave your audience may be short.
INDAMORA.

You need not fear I shall detain you long,
Yet you may tell me your pretended wrong.
AURENG-ZEBE.

Is that the bus'ness? Then my stay is vain.
INDAMORA.

How are you injured?
AURENG-ZEBE.   When did I complain?   460
INDAMORA.

Leave off your forced respect,
And show your rage in its most furious form;
I'm armed with innocence to brave the storm.
You heard, perhaps, your brother's last desire,
And after saw him in my arms expire,   465
Saw me with tears so great a loss bemoan,
Heard me complaining my last hopes were gone.
AURENG-ZEBE.

"Oh stay, and take me with you when you go;
There's nothing now worth living for below."
Unhappy sex, whose beauty is your snare,   470
Exposed to trials, made too frail to bear.
I grow a fool, and show my rage again;
'Tis nature's fault, and why should I complain?

452. never see] *Q 1–2, 4;* see *Q 3,*
5–6.

INDAMORA.

    Will you yet hear me?

AURENG-ZEBE.   Yes, till you relate

    What pow'rful motives did your change create.   475

    You thought me dead, and prudently did weigh

    Tears were but vain, and brought but youth's decay.

    Then, in Morat, your hopes a crown designed,

    And all the woman worked within your mind.

    I rave again, and to my rage return,   480

    To be again subjected to your scorn.

INDAMORA.

    I wait till this long storm be over-blown.

AURENG-ZEBE.

    I'm conscious of my folly: I have done.

    I cannot rail, but silently I'll grieve.

    How did I trust! And how did you deceive!   485

    Oh, Arimant, would I had died for thee!

    I dearly buy thy generosity.

INDAMORA.

    Alas, is he then dead?

AURENG-ZEBE.   Unknown to me

    He took my arms, and while I forced my way

    Through troops of foes which did our passage stay,   490

    My buckler o'er my aged father cast,

    Still fighting, still defending as I passed,

    The noble Arimant usurped my name,

    Fought, and took from me, while he gave me, fame.

    "To Aureng-Zebe!" he made his soldiers cry,   495

    And seeing not, where he heard danger nigh,

    Shot like a star through the benighted sky.

    A short but mighty aid; at length he fell.

    My own adventures 'twere lost time to tell,

    Or how my army, ent'ring in the night,   500

    Surprised our foes; the dark, disordered fight;

    How my appearance, and my father shown,

    Made peace, and all the rightful monarch own.

477. were but] *Q 1–2, 4*; but in
Q 3; were but in *Q 5–6*.

476. *weigh*] consider that.

I've summed it briefly, since it did relate
Th'unwelcome safety of the man you hate.   505

INDAMORA.

As briefly will I clear my innocence:
Your altered brother died in my defense.
Those tears you saw, that tenderness I showed,
Were just effects of grief and gratitude.
He died my convert.

AURENG-ZEBE.   But your lover too.   510
I heard his words, and did your actions view.
You seemed to mourn another lover dead;
My sighs you gave him, and my tears you shed.
But worst of all,
Your gratitude for his defense was shown;   515
It proved you valued life when I was gone.

INDAMORA.

Not that I valued life, but feared to die.
Think that my weakness, not inconstancy.

AURENG-ZEBE.

Fear showed you doubted of your own intent,
And he who doubts becomes less innocent.   520
Tell me not you could fear.
Fear's a large promiser; who subject live
To that base passion know not what they give.
No circumstance of grief you did deny,
And what could she give more who durst not die?   525

INDAMORA.

My love, my faith.

AURENG-ZEBE.   Both so adult'rate grown
When mixed with fear, they never could be known.
I wish no ill might her I love befall,
But she ne'er loved who durst not venture all.
Her life and fame should my concernment be,   530
But she should only be afraid for me.

INDAMORA.

My heart was yours, but oh, you left it here,
Abandoned to those tyrants, hope and fear.
If they forced from me one kind look or word,
Could you not that, not that small part afford?   535

AURENG-ZEBE.

    If you had loved, you nothing yours could call;
    Giving the least of mine, you gave him all.
    True love's a miser, so tenacious grown
    He weighs to the least grain of what's his own.
    More delicate than honor's nicest sense   540
    Neither to give nor take the least offense.
    With or without you I can have no rest;
    What shall I do? Y'are lodged within my breast;
    Your image never will be thence displaced,
    But there it lies, stabbed, mangled, and defaced.   545

INDAMORA.

    Yet to restore the quiet of your heart
    There's one way left.

AURENG-ZEBE.   Oh name it.

INDAMORA.   'Tis to part.

    Since perfect bliss with me you cannot prove,
    I scorn to bless by halves the man I love.

AURENG-ZEBE.

    Now you distract me more. Shall then the day   550
    Which views my triumph see our loves decay?
    Must I new bars to my own joy create?
    Refuse myself what I had forced from fate?
    What though I am not loved?
    Reason's nice taste does our delights destroy;   555
    Brutes are more blessed, who grossly feed on joy.

INDAMORA.

    Such endless jealousies your love pursue,
    I can no more be fully blessed than you.
    I therefore go, to free us both from pain.
    I prized your person, but your crown disdain.   560
    Nay, ev'n my own—
    I give it you; for since I cannot call
    My heart your subject, I'll not reign at all.   *Exit.*

549. bless] *Q 3, 6;* bliss *Q 1-2, 4-5.*   553. had] *Q 1-2, 4-6;* hard *Q 3.*
551. triumph] *Q 1-2;*   triumphs
Q 3-6.

539. *grain*] 1/480 ounce.
540. *nicest*] most scrupulous.
548. *prove*] attain.

AURENG-ZEBE.

Go! Though thou leav'st me tortured on the rack,
'Twixt shame and pride, I cannot call thee back.   565
She's guiltless, and I should submit, but oh!
When she exacts it, can I stoop so low?
Yes, for she's guiltless. But she's haughty too.
Great souls long struggle ere they own a crime;
She's gone, and leaves me no repenting time.   570
I'll call her now. Sure if she loves she'll stay;
Linger at least, or not go far away.
                              Looks to the door, and returns.
Forever lost, and I repent too late.
My foolish pride would set my whole estate,
Till at one throw I lost all back to fate.   575

         To him the Emperor, *drawing in* Indamora; *attendants.*

EMPEROR.

It must not be that he by whom we live
Should no advantage of his gift receive.
Should he be wholly wretched? He alone
In this blessed day, a day so much his own?—
(*To* Indamora.) I have not quitted yet a victor's right;   580
I'll make you happy in your own despite.
I love you still, and if I struggle hard
To give, it shows the worth of the reward.

INDAMORA.

Suppose he has o'ercome; must I find place
Among his conquered foes, and sue for grace?   585
Be pardoned, and confess I loved not well?
What though none live my innocence to tell?
I know it. Truth may own a gen'rous pride:
I clear myself, and care for none beside.

AURENG-ZEBE.

Oh Indamora, you would break my heart!   590
Could you resolve, on any terms, to part?
I thought your love eternal; was it tied
So loosely that a quarrel could divide?

574. *set*] wager.

> I grant that my suspicions were unjust,
> But would you leave me for a small distrust?   595
> Forgive these foolish words—   *Kneeling to her.*
> They were the froth my raging folly moved
> When it boiled up. I knew not then I loved,
> Yet then loved most.

INDAMORA (*to* Aureng-Zebe, *giving her hand, smiling*).
> You would but half be blessed!

AURENG-ZEBE.   Oh do but try   600
> My eager love; I'll give myself the lie.
> The very hope is a full happiness,
> Yet scantly measures what I shall possess.
> Fancy itself, ev'n in enjoyment, is
> But a dumb judge, and cannot tell its bliss.   605

EMPEROR.
> Her eyes a secret yielding do confess,
> And promise to partake your happiness.
> May all the joys I did myself pursue
> Be raised by her and multiplied on you.

[*Enter*] *a procession of priests, slaves following, and last* Melesinda, *in white.*

INDAMORA.
> Alas! What means this pomp?   610

AURENG-ZEBE.
> 'Tis the procession of a funeral vow,
> Which cruel laws to Indian wives allow
> When fatally their virtue they approve;
> Cheerful in flames, and martyrs of their love.

INDAMORA.
> Oh my foreboding heart! Th'event I fear.   615
> And see! Sad Melesinda does appear.

MELESINDA.
> You wrong my love; what grief do I betray?
> This is the triumph of my nuptial day.
> My better nuptials, which in spite of fate

603. scantly] *Q 1–2, 4–5;* scanty
Q 3, 6.

613. *approve*] demonstrate.

Forever join me to my dear Morat.   620
Now I am pleased; my jealousies are o'er:
He's mine, and I can lose him now no more.

EMPEROR.
Let no false show of fame your reason blind.

INDAMORA.
You have no right to die; he was not kind.

MELESINDA.
Had he been kind, I could no love have shown;   625
Each vulgar virtue would as much have done.
My love was such it needed no return,
But could, though he supplied no fuel, burn.
Rich in itself, like elemental fire,
Whose pureness does no aliment require.   630
In vain you would bereave me of my lord,
For I will die. Die is too base a word;
I'll seek his breast, and kindling by his side,
Adorned with flames, I'll mount a glorious bride.   *Exit.*

Enter Nourmahal, *distracted, with* Zayda.

ZAYDA.
She's lost, she's lost! But why do I complain   635
For her who generously did life disdain!
Poisoned, she raves;
Th'invenomed body does the soul attack;
Th'invenomed soul works its own poison back.

NOURMAHAL.
I burn! I more than burn; I am all fire!   640
See how my mouth and nostrils flame expire!
I'll not come near myself—
Now I'm a burning lake; it rolls and flows;
I'll rush and pour it all upon my foes.
Pull, pull that reverend piece of timber near;   645
Throw't on—'tis dry—'twill burn.
Ha, ha! How my old husband crackles there!
Keep him down, keep him down, turn him about;
I know him; he'll but whiz and straight go out.

---

630. *aliment*] nourishment.
649. *whiz*] hiss.

Fan me, you winds! What, not one breath of air? 650
I burn 'em all, and yet have flames to spare.
Quench me; pour on whole rivers. 'Tis in vain:
Morat stands there to drive 'em back again.
With those huge bellows in his hands he blows
New fire into my head; my brain-pan glows. 655
See, see! There's Aureng-Zebe too takes his part;
But he blows all his fire into my heart.

AURENG-ZEBE.
Alas, what fury's this?

NOURMAHAL (*staring upon him and catching at him*).
          That's he, that's he!
I know the dear man's voice.
And this my rival, this the cursed she. 660
They kiss; into each other's arms they run,
Close, close, close! Must I see, and must have none?
Thou art not hers; give me that eager kiss!
Ingrateful! Have I lost Morat for this?
Will you? Before my face? Poor helpless I 665
See all, and have my hell before I die!   *Sinks down.*

EMPEROR.
With thy last breath thou hast thy crimes confessed.
Farewell; and take what thou ne'er gav'st me, rest.
But you, my son, receive it better here:
          Giving him Indamora's hand.
The just rewards of love and honor wear. 670
Receive the mistress you so long have served;
Receive the crown your loyalty preserved.
Take you the reins, while I from cares remove,
And sleep within the chariot which I drove.

          [*Exeunt.*]

674.1. *Exeunt*] *Q 3, 6; om. Q 1–2,*
4–5.

Epilogue

A pretty task! And so I told the fool
Who needs would undertake to please by rule.
He thought that if his characters were good;
The scenes entire, and freed from noise and blood;
The action great, yet circumscribed by time;   5
The words not forced, but sliding into rhyme;
The passions raised and calmed by just degrees,
As tides are swelled and then retire to seas—
He thought, in hitting these, his bus'ness done,
Though he perhaps has failed in every one.   10
But after all a poet must confess
His art's like physic, but a happy guess.
Your pleasure on your fancy must depend:
The lady's pleased just as she likes her friend.
No song! no dance! no show! he fears you'll say;   15
You love all naked beauties but a play.
He much mistakes your methods to delight,
And like the French, abhors our target-fight;
But those damned dogs can never be i'th' right.
True English hate your Monsieur's paltry arts,   20
For you are all silk weavers in your hearts.
Bold Britons at a brave bear-garden fray
Are roused, and clatt'ring sticks, cry, "Play, play, play!"
Meantime, your filthy foreigner will stare
And mutter to himself, "Ha! *Gens barbare!*"   25
And gad, 'tis well he mutters—well for him;
Our butchers else would tear him limb from limb.
'Tis true, the time may come your sons may be
Infected with this French civility,
But this in after ages will be done;   30

---

12. art's] *Q 1-2, 4-6*; art *Q 3.*

4. *entire*] complete, continuous.
17. *He . . . delight*] He misunderstands your kind of entertainment.
21. *For . . . hearts*] Scott-Saintsbury interprets *you* as referring to the audience, seen as champions of English manufactures against the French imports. It is also possible that the pronoun refers to the French in a directly derogatory manner.
25. *Gens barbare*] barbarians.

Our poet writes a hundred years too soon.
This age comes on too slow, or he too fast,
And early springs are subject to a blast.
Who would excel, when few can make a test
Betwixt indiff'rent writing and the best?   35
For favors cheap and common who would strive,
Which, like abandoned prostitutes, you give?
Yet scattered here and there I some behold
Who can discern the tinsel from the gold.
To these he writes; and if by them allowed,   40
'Tis their prerogative to rule the crowd.
For he more fears (like a presuming man)
Their votes who cannot judge, than theirs who can.

FINIS

Appendix

Chronology

Approximate dates are indicated by *. Dates for plays are those on which they were first made public, either on stage or in print.

Political and Literary Events	*Life and Works of John Dryden*
1631	
Death of Donne.	Born August 9.
1633	
Samuel Pepys born.	
1635	
Sir George Etherege born.*	
1640	
Aphra Behn born.*	
1641	
William Wycherley born.*	
1642	
First Civil War began (ended 1646).	
Theaters closed by Parliament.	
Thomas Shadwell born.*	
1644	
	Attended Westminster School, 1644*–1650*.
1648	
Second Civil War.	
Nathaniel Lee born.*	
1649	
Execution of Charles I.	
1650	
Jeremy Collier born.	
1651	
Hobbes' *Leviathan* published.	
1652	
First Dutch War began (ended 1654).	

Thomas Otway born.
1654

B.A., Trinity College, Cambridge.
in March.

1656
D'Avenant's *THE SIEGE OF
RHODES* performed at Rutland
House.
1657
John Dennis born.
1658
Death of Oliver Cromwell.
D'Avenant's *THE CRUELTY OF
THE SPANIARDS IN PERU* per-
formed at the Cockpit.
1659

Heroic Stanzas published.

1660
Restoration of Charles II.
Theatrical patents granted to
Thomas Killigrew and Sir William
D'Avenant, authorizing them to
form, respectively, the King's and
the Duke of York's Companies.
Pepys began his diary.
1661
Cowley's *THE CUTTER OF
COLEMAN STREET.*
D'Avenant's *THE SIEGE OF
RHODES* (expanded to two parts).
1662
Charter granted to the Royal
Society.
1663
Tuke's *THE ADVENTURES OF
FIVE HOURS.*

Astraea Redux published.

THE WILD GALLANT produced
in February at Vere Street.
Married Lady Elizabeth Howard
on December 1.

1664
Sir John Vanbrugh born.
Etherege's *THE COMICAL
REVENGE.*

THE INDIAN QUEEN, with Sir
Robert Howard, produced in January at Bridges Street.

THE RIVAL LADIES produced in June* at Bridges Street.

1665

Second Dutch War began (ended 1667).
Great Plague.
Orrery's *MUSTAPHA*.

THE INDIAN EMPEROR produced in May* at Bridges Street.

1666

Fire of London.
Death of James Shirley.

1667

Jonathan Swift born.
Milton's *Paradise Lost* published.
Sprat's *The History of the Royal Society* published.

Annus Mirabilis published in January.
SECRET LOVE, OR THE MAIDEN QUEEN produced in March* at Bridges Street.
SIR MARTIN MAR-ALL, OR THE FEIGNED INNOCENCE, with the Duke of Newcastle, produced in August at Lincoln's Inn Fields.
THE TEMPEST, OR THE ENCHANTED ISLAND, with Sir William Davenant, produced in November at Lincoln's Inn Fields.

1668

Death of D'Avenant.
Shadwell's *THE SULLEN LOVERS*.

Appointed Poet Laureate in April.
Essay of Dramatic Poesy published.
AN EVENING'S LOVE, OR THE MOCK ASTROLOGER produced in June at Bridges Street.

1669

Pepys terminated his diary.
Susanna Centlivre born.

TYRANNIC LOVE, OR THE ROYAL MARTYR produced in June at Bridges Street.

1670

William Congreve born.

Appointed Historiographer Royal.
THE CONQUEST OF GRANADA BY THE SPANIARDS, Part I, produced in December at Bridges Street.

1671

Dorset Garden Theatre (Duke's Company) opened.

THE CONQUEST OF GRANADA BY THE SPANIARDS, Part II

Colley Cibber born.
Milton's *Paradise Regained* and *Samson Agonistes* published.
THE REHEARSAL, by the Duke of Buckingham and others.
Wycherley's *LOVE IN A WOOD*.

produced in January at Bridges Street.

1672
Third Dutch War began (ended 1674).
Joseph Addison born.
Richard Steele born.

MARRIAGE A LA MODE produced in April* at Lincoln's Inn Fields.
THE ASSIGNATION, OR LOVE IN A NUNNERY produced in October at Lincoln's Inn Fields.

1673

AMBOYNA produced at Lincoln's Inn Fields.*

1674
New Drury Lane Theatre (King's Company) opened.
Death of Milton.
Nicholas Rowe born.
Thomas Rymer's *Reflections on Aristotle's Treatise of Poesy* (translation of Rapin) published.

THE STATE OF INNOCENCE published.

1675
Wycherley's *THE COUNTRY WIFE*.*

AURENG-ZEBE produced in November at Drury Lane.

1676
Etherege's *THE MAN OF MODE*.
Otway's *DON CARLOS*.
Shadwell's *THE VIRTUOSO*.
Wycherley's *THE PLAIN DEALER*.

1677
Rymer's *Tragedies of the Last Age Considered* published.
Aphra Behn's *THE ROVER*.
Lee's *THE RIVAL QUEENS*.

ALL FOR LOVE, OR THE WORLD WELL LOST produced in December at Drury Lane.

1678
Popish Plot.
George Farquhar born.
Bunyan's *Pilgrim's Progress* (Part I) published.

THE KIND KEEPER, OR MR. LIMBERHAM produced in March at Dorset Garden.

1679

Exclusion Bill introduced.
Death of Thomas Hobbes.
Death of Roger Boyle, Earl of Orrery.
Charles Johnson born.

TROILUS AND CRESSIDA, OR TRUTH FOUND TOO LATE produced in April* at Dorset Garden.

1680

Death of Samuel Butler.
Death of John Wilmot, Earl of Rochester.
Lee's *LUCIUS JUNIUS BRUTUS.*
Otway's *THE ORPHAN.*

Ovid's Epistles published.
THE SPANISH FRIAR, OR THE DOUBLE DISCOVERY produced in March at Dorset Garden.

1681

Charles II dissolved Parliament at Oxford.
Tate's adaptation of *KING LEAR.*

Absalom and Achitophel published in November.

1682

The King's and the Duke of York's Companies merged into the United Company.
Otway's *VENICE PRESERVED.*

The Medal published in March.
MacFlecknoe published in October.
THE DUKE OF GUISE, with Nathaniel Lee, produced in November at Drury Lane.
Religio Laici published in November.

1683

Rye House Plot.
Death of Thomas Killigrew.
Crowne's *CITY POLITIQUES.*

1684

Miscellany Poems published.

1685

Death of Charles II; accession of James II.
Revocation of the Edict of Nantes.
The Duke of Monmouth's Rebellion.
Death of Otway.
John Gay born.
Crowne's *SIR COURTLY NICE.*

Became a Roman Catholic.
Sylvae published in January.
ALBION AND ALBANIUS produced in June at Dorset Garden.

1687

Death of the Duke of Buckingham.
Newton's *Principia* published.

The Hind and the Panther published in May.

1688

The Revolution.

Alexander Pope born.
Shadwell's *THE SQUIRE OF ALSATIA.*

1689
The War of the League of Augsburg began (ended 1697).
Toleration Act.
Death of Aphra Behn.
Shadwell made Poet Laureate.
Shadwell's *BURY FAIR.*

DON SEBASTIAN, KING OF PORTUGAL produced in December at Drury Lane.

1690
Battle of the Boyne.
Locke's *Two Treatises of Government* and *An Essay Concerning Human Understanding* published.

AMPHITRYON, OR THE TWO SOSIAS produced in October at Drury Lane.

1691
Death of Etherege.*
Langbaine's *An Account of the English Dramatic Poets* published.

KING ARTHUR, OR THE BRITISH WORTHY produced in May* at Dorset Garden.

1692
Death of Lee.
Death of Shadwell.
Tate made Poet Laureate.

CLEOMENES, THE SPARTAN HERO produced in April at Drury Lane.
The Satires of Juvenal and Persius published in October.

1693
George Lillo born.*
Rymer's *A Short View of Tragedy* published.
Congreve's *THE OLD BACHELOR.*

1694
Death of Queen Mary.
Southerne's *THE FATAL MARRIAGE.*

LOVE TRIUMPHANT, OR NATURE WILL PREVAIL produced in January at Drury Lane.

1695
Group of actors led by Thomas Betterton left Drury Lane and established a new company at Lincoln's Inn Fields.
Congreve's *LOVE FOR LOVE.*
Southerne's *OROONOKO.*

1696
Cibber's *LOVE'S LAST SHIFT*.
Vanbrugh's *THE RELAPSE*.

1697
Treaty of Ryswick ended the War of the League of Augsburg.
Charles Macklin born.
Congreve's *THE MOURNING BRIDE*.
Vanbrugh's *THE PROVOKED WIFE*.

The Works of Vergil published in June.

1698
Collier controversy started with the publication of *A Short View of the Immorality and Profaneness of the English Stage*.

1699
Farquhar's *THE CONSTANT COUPLE*.

1700
Blackmore's *Satire against Wit* published.
Congreve's *THE WAY OF THE WORLD*.

Fables Ancient and Modern published in March.
Died May 1; buried in Westminster Abbey.

1701
Act of Settlement.
War of the Spanish Succession began (ended 1713).
Death of James II.
Rowe's *TAMERLANE*.
Steele's *THE FUNERAL*.

1702
Death of William III; accession of Anne.
The Daily Courant began publication.
Cibber's *SHE WOULD AND SHE WOULD NOT*.

1703
Death of Samuel Pepys.
Rowe's *THE FAIR PENITENT*.

1704
Capture of Gibraltar; Battle of Blenheim.

Defoe's *The Review* began publication (1704–1713).
Swift's *A Tale of a Tub* and *The Battle of the Books* published.
Cibber's *THE CARELESS HUSBAND*.

1705
Haymarket Theatre opened.
Steele's *THE TENDER HUSBAND*.

1706
Battle of Ramillies.
Farquhar's *THE RECRUITING OFFICER*.

1707
Union of Scotland and England.
Death of Farquhar.
Henry Fielding born.
Farquhar's *THE BEAUX' STRATAGEM*.

1708
Downes' *Roscius Anglicanus* published.

1709
Samuel Johnson born.
Rowe's edition of Shakespeare published.
The Tatler began publication (1709–1711).
Centlivre's *THE BUSY BODY*.

1711
Shaftesbury's *Characteristics* published.
The Spectator began publication (1711–1712).
Pope's *An Essay on Criticism* published.

1713
Treaty of Utrecht ended the War of the Spanish Succession.
Addison's *CATO*.

1714
Death of Anne; accession of George
I.
Steele became Governor of Drury
Lane.
John Rich assumed management
of Lincoln's Inn Fields.
Centlivre's *THE WONDER: A
WOMAN KEEPS A SECRET.*
Rowe's *JANE SHORE.*

1715
Jacobite Rebellion.
Death of Tate.
Rowe made Poet Laureate.
Death of Wycherley.

1716
Addison's *THE DRUMMER.*

1717
David Garrick born.
Cibber's *THE NON-JUROR.*
Gay, Pope, and Arbuthnot's
*THREE HOURS AFTER
MARRIAGE.*

1718
Death of Rowe.
Centlivre's *A BOLD STROKE FOR
A WIFE.*

1719
Death of Addison.
Defoe's *Robinson Crusoe* published.
Young's *BUSIRIS, KING OF
EGYPT.*

1720
South Sea Bubble.
Samuel Foote born.
Steele suspended from the Gover-
norship of Drury Lane (restored
1721).
Little Theatre in the Haymarket
opened.
Steele's *The Theatre* (periodical)
published.

Hughes' *THE SIEGE OF DAMAS-CUS.*

1721

Walpole became first Minister.

1722

Steele's *THE CONSCIOUS LOVERS.*

1723

Death of Susanna Centlivre.

Death of D'Urfey.

1725

Pope's edition of Shakespeare published.

1726

Death of Jeremy Collier.

Death of Vanbrugh.

Law's *Unlawfulness of Stage Entertainments* published.

Swift's *Gulliver's Travels* published.

1727

Death of George I; accession of George II.

Death of Sir Isaac Newton.

Arthur Murphy born.

1728

Pope's *The Dunciad* (first version) published.

Cibber's *THE PROVOKED HUSBAND* (expansion of Vanbrugh's fragment *A JOURNEY TO LONDON*).

Gay's *THE BEGGAR'S OPERA.*

1729

Goodman's Fields Theatre opened.

Death of Congreve.

Death of Steele.

Edmund Burke born.

1730

Cibber made Poet Laureate.

Oliver Goldsmith born.

Thomson's *The Seasons* published.

Fielding's *THE AUTHOR'S FARCE.*

Fielding's *TOM THUMB* (revised

as *THE TRAGEDY OF TRAGED-
IES*, 1731).

1731
Death of Defoe.
Fielding's *THE GRUB-STREET
OPERA*.
Lillo's *THE LONDON MER-
CHANT*.

1732
Covent Garden Theatre opened.
Death of Gay.
George Colman the elder born.
Fielding's *THE CONVENT GAR-
DEN TRAGEDY*.
Fielding's *THE MODERN HUS-
BAND*.
Charles Johnson's *CAELIA*.

1733
Pope's *An Essay on Man* (Epistles
I–III) published (Epistle IV, 1734).

1734
Death of Dennis.
The Prompter began publication
(1734–1736).
Theobald's edition of Shakespeare
published.
Fielding's *DON QUIXOTE IN
ENGLAND*.

1736
Fielding led the "Great Mogul's
Company of Comedians" at the
Little Theatre in the Haymarket
(1736–1737).
Fielding's *PASQUIN*.
Lillo's *FATAL CURIOSITY*.

1737
The Stage Licensing Act.
Dodsley's *THE KING AND THE
MILLER OF MANSFIELD*.
Fielding's *THE HISTORICAL
REGISTER FOR 1736*.